Waiting on Halley's Comet

Waiting

on Halley's Comet

Short-Story Snapshots of the Human Spirit

John M. Eades, Ph.D.

Health Communications, Inc.
Deerfield Beach, Florida
www.hci-online.com

Library of Congress Cataloging-in-Publication Data

Eades, John M.
    Waiting on Halley's comet : short-story snapshots of the human
spirit / John M. Eades.
        p.   cm.
    ISBN 1-55874-514-9 (pbk.)
    1. Conduct of life.   2. Christian life.   I. Title
BJ1597.E33   1997
813'.54—dc21   97-14602
                                                                       CIP

Publisher: Health Communications, Inc.
                   3201 S.W. 15th Street
                   Deerfield Beach, Florida 33442-8190

Cover design by Andrea Perrine Brower

This book is dedicated to the memory of
Joseph Woody Eades.

Contents

Acknowledgments

I am grateful for my loving family, who has stood by me through all the trials and errors of life.

A special thanks is due to Billy Lyon, a friend who has believed in me and rescued me from the brink of ruin more than once in my life. Without his support, this book would never have been written. The same is true of Charlie Fleming, a man for all seasons, who was there in fair weather and foul.

This book was born of my search for serenity and a deeper spirituality. I am indebted to Reverend Jon Bell, who has led me from the wilderness with his wisdom and the gentle grace of God.

To my Tennessee friends, who healed my heart and encouraged me in the completion of this book—God bless you. My warmest appreciation goes to: Ron Bailey, who knows that even angels have skinned knees; Judge Buddy Perry, who is wise in common sense and wonderful in his compassion; James Chandler, a fellow writer and retired army colonel, who is intimately familiar with the battles of war as well as those of the soul.

Gentlemen, you are cherished, as are your wives, Debra, Jean and Sylvia.

Last but most, I am eternally grateful that God has allowed this prodigal son to come home.

Introduction

After my first book, *The 7th Floor Ain't Too High for Angels to Fly*, I faced a thought that had been tailgating my mind as I traveled the well-worn path of my life. Frankly, I didn't like what I saw.

I didn't want to admit it, but working in the field of addiction for over two decades had taken its toll. My soul was shattered from the daily collisions against the walls erected by most addicts so that they could continue in their self-destructive disease. There was ample evidence that my soul needed a sabbatical to renew itself. The thought was like a tune that I couldn't get out of my mind. I knew I couldn't continue to be a wallflower, so I decided to dance with this dilemma.

I couldn't afford to relinquish financial security to pursue the mending of my soul which, ironically, had broken in the process of helping others fix theirs. However, I couldn't afford not to, if that's what it took. I had made the same transition that occurs in the lives of many idealists. As I aged, I had gone from thinking I could save the world to thinking I could at least save some, to realizing that if I wasn't careful I couldn't even save myself. It had taken me a little more than half a century to heed the caveat of Christ: "For what is a man profited if he gains the whole world, and loses his own soul?"

Well, I sure was a long way from gaining the whole world, but just around the corner from losing the ragged remains of my soul. Acknowledging this, I took a leap of faith and stepped down from my job. To me, this step seemed as big as that one the astronauts made on the moon—or at least, the gravity of my situation was greater. (I gave up my job, not my sense of humor.)

It is really strange how your friends react when you step out onto the ledge of life to let the fresh air flow into your soul. They think you have lost your mind and are going to jump before they can convince you to crawl back inside where it is safe but stifling to your spirit. They finally understand I am on borrowed time, and borrowed money I might add, and before long I'll return to the world of work once again. At last, they have folded up their safety nets and wished me well.

I have spent the last several months writing these stories and searching for spirituality. I am not certain of the progress that has been made in each endeavor, but I have found serenity in the effort.

Most of these stories are rooted in reality, but some are the product of literary license. They are written to inspire, instruct, enlighten and entertain. Some of the stories won't necessarily make you feel good, but, hopefully, they will make you feel—and think. Emotional numbness is the terrible malady of our times, but perhaps these offerings will awaken your heart, especially to all the goodness inside of you.

As I stated in my previous book, I surely don't have

the answers to life's problems, and I doubt that any therapists do. However, I do not doubt the words of William James, the famed Harvard psychologist, who said, "Permanent change only comes when a person has a spiritual transformation."

The truth is, most of us are not as good as all our friends think we are or as bad as all our enemies claim. We are just fellow travelers and searchers along this road of life who sometimes get tired and lost, and need to stop and brush off the dust of our daily disappointments as we rechart our course. Rest up and read for a while, the journey will wait. Maybe what you are searching for is just around the bend of your heart.

1
Wash Day

What we have done for ourselves alone
dies with us. What we have done for
others and the world remains and is
immortal.

Albert Pine

Joe Hill was the town drunk. In the summertime, I would sit on the screened-in porch with Grandma as she rocked and shelled peas and sang hymns. She sang in a way that made me think that maybe God was hidden somewhere up in the huge oak tree that shaded the front yard, listening to every sweet word she sang. In those days, you rarely saw a man strolling through the neighborhood in the daytime on a weekday unless he was retired or disabled in some way, or was either the postman or a deliveryman. Therefore, whenever a man appeared in the distance walking toward Grandma's house at midday, I always thought it was Mr. Hill, and I was usually right.

It was a Thursday. That is easy to remember because that was linen day, when Grandma washed all the sheets and pillowcases and hung them on the metal clothesline in the backyard to dry. I always helped her, but after a summer of dropping one end of the sheets on the ground every time I tried to hang one up, she put me in charge of hanging nothing but pillowcases. Still, I felt important because those pieces of cotton seemed just about the most important business there was, or at least Grandma made it seem that way. The wrinkles caused by the damp clothes had just about disappeared from my fingers, and now we were on the front porch when I saw what appeared to be Mr. Hill swaying from side to side as he came down the street.

It was him all right. He was dressed in baggy cotton pants held up with a too-long belt that flopped down and around in front like a worn-out dog's tongue. His long-sleeved white shirt had a yellow tinge to it, and the cuffs were about six inches from his wrist and not buttoned. He was in need of a good shave and a haircut, and it seemed the most redeeming article he had on was a gold watch fob with one end attached to a belt loop in front of his pants, while the other end descended deep into his right front pocket. He stopped on the sidewalk in front of the house and looked up toward the screened porch. Then he spoke. "Good day, Mrs. Allen. I was just out walking and thought I'd stop by and say hello to you and your grandson."

"I'm so glad you came by, Mr. Hill," Grandma said as she set the pan of shelled peas down on the porch. "I wonder if you would be kind enough to tell me what time it is?" He stood as erect as his wobbly legs would allow. "I sure will!" he replied, as he let his hand follow the chain down into his pocket. He removed the watch with a flair and popped open the protective case. In a refined voice he said, "It is exactly 1:27 and 32 seconds." It was obvious to me that Mr. Hill was extremely proud of his watch.

"Thank you so much, Mr. Hill. That sure is a mighty fine watch you have there," Grandma politely said, as he began putting the watch back in his pocket—although it took him several attempts before it was once again safely tucked into his right front pocket. He turned to continue on his way when Grandma called out to him.

"Oh, Mr. Hill, I was just wondering if you could come by tomorrow and cut the grass in my backyard. It's getting so high back there that I can hardly hang my sheets without getting grass stains on them. I'll pay you three dollars and give you all the peas and cornbread you can eat. You sure would be doing me a big favor if you would say yes."

Now Mr. Hill stood even taller as he rubbed his chin as though he were in deep thought. "Well, Mrs. Allen, I guess if you really need that grass cut, then I'll be happy to oblige. I'll be here at 7:30 in the morning before it gets too hot." Once again, Mr. Hill turned to continue on his way. His first step seemed to have great life in it, almost like a band major beginning to lead out the band in a fine march.

He had taken several more jaunty strides when Grandma quickly rose to her feet, pushed the screen door open, and yelled loud enough for all the other neighbors on their porches to hear. "Mr. Hill, please come back here a minute, would you?" He turned as precisely as a drill sergeant and returned until he was even with the cobblestone walk that led up to the front porch. It didn't seem Grandma knew how close he was, for she continued to speak in an extremely loud voice.

"Thank you for coming back, Mr. Hill. I was wondering if you had the time to do an old lady one more huge favor?" Mr. Hill once again started to take out his watch, then caught himself when he sheepishly realized she wasn't asking him for the time again. He quickly regained his composure.

"I'm in no hurry, Mrs. Allen. What can I do for you?" he said, using that refined voice once again.

"Mr. Hill," Grandma said, in a voice so loud that I wondered if Mr. Hill might be going deaf, "Mr. Allen, before he passed, always said you were the best whistler in this entire town. He once told me he heard you whistle "Amazing Grace" and said it was the most beautiful thing he had ever heard in all his life. It sure would make me mighty happy if you would whistle it for me. Would you please do that for me?"

Mr. Hill didn't say a word. He just pulled himself up

even higher, until he seemed to stand about as tall as the giant oak tree in the front yard, and began whistling. Grandma's neighbors had stopped what they were doing, and they listened just like we did. It was beautiful. After he had finished, Grandma clapped her hands in a show of great appreciation for Mr. Hill. His smile seemed to stretch the entire length of the sidewalk.

"Thank you so very much, Mr. Hill," she said. "We'll be expecting you tomorrow morning. Have a wonderful day!"

Mr. Hill waved good-bye and walked away so much taller and prouder than when he came. It was wash day, all right. My Grandma was a most wise woman who, for a moment in time, had washed away the ground-in dirt that had soiled Mr. Hill's soul for many years. Chances were that by the next Thursday he would be soiled again, but on this particular day he was washed clean.

2

I Ain't Jesus, I'm Just the Janitor

You do not see the river of mourning because it lacks one tear of your own.

Antonio Porchia

A cold body is not shameful; a cold heart is.

Anonymous

Abraham Jemison was the custodian at a small church in the city. The church sat right on the corner. It was a local landmark and was listed in the historical register.

It was the church where Abraham swept and dusted and polished on the inside, and mowed and trimmed the grass and shrubs on the outside. By each Saturday evening, he had made everything immaculate for the Sunday service. Then he locked the doors, went home and laid out his clothes for church the next day.

His own church, the one he went to, was located far out in the country, and he had to get up early to make it to Sunday school on time, which he always did without fail. For the last seven years, Abraham had a perfect attendance record at his church, which wasn't bad for a retired high school janitor in his late 60s. Beneath his gray hair and eyebrows, Abraham's body had the stamina and strength of a younger man, with these physical assets springing from years of hard work and right living. He was a good man for sure they say, or at least he was until that freezing Wednesday night in November, the night before Thanksgiving in 1976.

The prayer service at the city church was over, and Abraham had come by to clean up a little, then lock the doors and go home. He pulled up into the parking lot of the beautiful old church and got out of his rusty pickup truck just as the minister was coming out of his study to head home.

"Good evening, Abraham," Dr. Parks said, pulling on

his gloves. "I sure hope your truck has a good heater. Weatherman says it's going down to 17 degrees tonight. Hard freeze, he says. Be sure to wrap the outside faucets and leave the water dripping in the kitchen so the pipes won't burst."

"I sure will, Dr. Parks," Abraham answered, the cold night air causing clouds to come with his words. "I reckon ya'll had a good prayer meeting?"

Dr. Parks smiled. "Indeed we did, Abraham. Tonight we prayed for the homeless that on a night such as this they may find shelter and food. We also said our prayers to God for all the blessings we have to be thankful for this season. It was an excellent night all around," Dr. Parks said as he unlocked his car. "Well, happy Thanksgiving, Abraham, and keep warm."

"Same to you, Dr. Parks!" Abraham shouted, with a good-bye wave as he hurried on inside the church to escape the bitterly cold wind.

Abraham was a fast worker. He cleaned the kitchen first, remembering to leave the faucet running, then started on the main sanctuary. He saved the outside faucets for last, and he wrapped them securely with old rags. With all his work completed, he unsnapped the big ring of keys from his belt, found the right one and locked the side door. "These ain't the keys to the kingdom, but they shore is a mess of keys," he chuckled to himself, as the wind howled through the swaying pines around the church. Now, all Abraham had to do was get in his old truck and head home. If he had, he might still be the custodian at the church. But he didn't.

As he stood in the parking lot, Dr. Parks's remarks about the homeless came back to Abraham, as though the words themselves had been frozen and were waiting in the parking lot for Abraham to return and thaw them out with his presence. Suddenly, Abraham had an idea, maybe even a revelation, that came to him as fast as the temperature was dropping. He knew what to do.

He found the key to the church bus, a refurbished school bus painted white with the church's name lettered on the side, cranked it up and before long was headed toward downtown. Abraham may not have been the smartest man in town, but he knew where the homeless, the hungry, the broken and the outcasts gathered.

He drove to the city parks, the bus stations, the post offices, the train yards, the vacant buildings, the concrete catacombs beneath the overpasses and the vacant lots where flames rose from rusted-out barrels filled with anything that would burn, casting eerie shadows on the people huddled around them trying to stay warm. Each place he stopped, Abraham made a simple proclamation: "If you want a warm place to sleep and hot food for your stomach, come with me!"

That was all it took to load that bus. The little sign up above the driver's seat said the bus capacity was 60 passengers, but 71 homeless people and an old black man named Abraham pulled into that historic church parking lot that freezing Wednesday night. A ship of fools, a cynic might have said, with Abraham as their captain. But it didn't matter; they had found a refuge in a time of trouble.

Abraham flicked on the lights and held open the side door as they filed into the church. In they came, black and white, yellow and red, a rainbow of people with no pot of gold. They were nobody and yet everybody. As they shuffled by, a white-haired old woman with one eye set down her green garbage bag stuffed with all her earthly possessions and asked, "Is this your church?"

"Oh, no, ma'am," Abraham replied, "but I do know it's

God's church, and He wouldn't want you cold and hungry on a night like this." She managed a smile, adjusted
the patch on her eye, then hoisted her green garbage
bag and entered the church.

The last person in this line of modern-day lepers was
a young man with an old face. He was talking loudly to
himself, and his dirty face made his wild eyes appear
even more frightening. Obviously he had some kind of
mental problem. All of a sudden, he fell to his knees
right there in front of a startled Abraham. "Jesus, Jesus,
you must be Jesus!" he cried out, as he cocked his head
to one side, looking up with fear in his eyes at Abraham.

Abraham's smile grew until it was even bigger than
the man's eyes. Then, lifting the man up to his feet, he
calmly said, "I ain't Jesus, I'm just the janitor. And
because you're the last one in, you're gonna be the first
one fed." Abraham gently put his arm around the now
silent young man and ushered him into the church, closing the door on the cold darkness and the disturbed
man's demons.

Abraham switched on the rest of the lights, turned up
the heat and got the coffee urn going. He then turned
on the stove, emptied the refrigerator, and began to fry
fish, bacon and hamburgers. Before he was through, he
had used up every morsel of food in that entire kitchen.
No short-order cook anywhere ever moved as fast as he
did that night. Abraham blessed the food as he cooked,
knowing the power of hunger and forgetfulness.

The warmth and full stomachs joined hands to gently
rock those weary souls to sleep that night. Most of them
slept on the padded pews that evening, while a few
who had sleeping bags slept in the aisles. It was quite a
sight, and before long even Abraham drifted off to sleep.

The next morning, after coffee, Abraham once again

loaded them on the bus and took them to the downtown mission, where they could eat a Thanksgiving meal
for free. It was there that a church member, doing volunteer work, saw Abraham driving the bus. Well, it wasn't
long before there was an inquiry into exactly what had
happened that night. Abraham, being an honest man,
told the absolute truth.

Although Dr. Parks pleaded and spoke Scripture in
Abraham's defense, it was useless. The church board
made its decision. Abraham was fired, instructed to pay
for the food to avoid prosecution and ordered to turn in
his keys. He was sad for a little while, but sadness
doesn't last very long for a man like Abraham, who has
the *real* keys to the Kingdom dangling from his heart.

3
Grandma and Her Garden

Wisdom has its root in goodness, and
not goodness its root in wisdom.

Emerson

Grandma Allen was of Cherokee heritage. She was tall, with high cheekbones and high morals. Her parents were more interested in raising crops than in raising her, so her formal education stopped when she was old enough to work in the fields. Somehow, she taught herself how to read books. Even more amazingly, she learned how to read people also.

For years, my parents' marriage stood in the white-water current of chaos until finally they gave up. Their love was swept away and broken into small fragments on the rocks of the reality they had perilously avoided for years. That reality was that they couldn't live together in peace. I took advantage of Grandma's open door and open arms policy. I went to live with her.

At this time of my life, I was a senior in high school but a first-grader when it came to life. I had the usual doses of adolescent insecurity and grandiosity, and a firm conviction that I was the ugliest guy in my high school. I played sports, and most of my good feelings about myself came from my athletic abilities. I had a real fear of conflict and angry people, for those were the responses I learned from my childhood. When I stepped onto Grandma's front porch, I had more baggage than the suitcase I carried.

Grandma greeted me like a prodigal son, even though I was too innocent and naïve to qualify as one. She made a big fuss over me, as they used to say, and squeezed me so hard the bones in my back popped out loud. I felt lost when I arrived, and Grandma made me feel found. But above all, she had made me feel claimed. I was her grandson, and she made it seem as if she had lived her whole life preparing for this moment—and now it was here. Home really is where the heart is, and Grandma Allen's white frame house became my home.

My senior year ran past me like a rabbit. I remember Grandma sitting on the top row of the bleachers in the gym watching me play basketball. She knew nothing at all about basketball, but she walked 13 blocks to see me play anyhow. And we walked home together after the game. I always felt honored, never embarrassed, to be seen with her. She was a woman of great character and dignity, and my classmates always treated her with respect. Charisma is a firefly, while character is a beacon. Grandma's light never flickered.

Grandma Allen did understand baseball, and come spring she was there for every game, with her fold-up lawn chair. She tended her garden and me that spring, and we both grew and flourished. She knew about roots and tilled the soil of my soul and worked hard planting the right seeds. As I write this, one of my deepest regrets is that I neglected so many of the beautiful ideas she sowed.

I suppose I remember Grandma Allen more for the roots she tried to give me than the rooting she did at sporting events, although she yelled as loud as anybody I've ever heard. By the time I came to live under her roof and next to her heart, she had narrowed her reading down to the daily newspaper and the Bible. God was a permanent boarder at Grandma's. Seems she had invited Him to come live there before I was even born, and she told me of the agreement she had with Him. He'd live with her, and when it was all over, she'd go live with Him. It was simple. She believed it and never swayed.

One afternoon before dark, we were sitting in the swing. She was reading the Bible, and I was scanning the sports pages. Soon I would be leaving to play professional baseball, and she and God would be the only two left there. "You be a good boy, Johnny," she said, "and behave yourself up there."

"I will, Grandma," I assured her.

"And remember the commandments, and don't break them," she instructed.

"I won't, Grandma," I answered her.

"And remember the Golden Rule," she told me, as though I were making my first parachute jump from an airplane and she were my sergeant, going over the last-minute instructions. "And don't ever forget the difference between right and wrong," she went on, "and always treat people with respect and kindness."

"I will, Grandma, I promise," I answered.

"And don't ever forget that I love you, Johnny, and I'll be a-praying for you."

"I know you will, Grandma," I said, as the sky turned to a red tint on the horizon.

The next morning I left with the same suitcase I had brought. I sure wish I had taken all the wisdom she imparted to me that spring evening, but I didn't. It wasn't just that I had left Grandma's words behind, but also those of her other Boarder. I was too wet behind the ears to realize all the curves that life would throw.

It is fair to say I have struck out more times than I have hit home runs in this game of life, and the ninth inning isn't that far off anymore. Looking back, I imagine experience isn't much more than experiencing what you wish you hadn't experienced, and not as good a teacher as Grandma after all.

Many years have passed since that long-ago spring

evening, and these days I'm busy searching for all those seeds that Grandma planted. I may not find all the roots, but this time I'm down on my knees, where I know I'll have a better chance of finding them. I am certain that Grandma Allen is now a permanent boarder in God's house and sometimes, if I'm real quiet, I can still hear her strong voice rooting loudly for me.

4

Lefty Gets It Right

Some people do good things in secret.
Sometimes it is even a secret to them,
this goodness that they have done.

Anonymous

He was called "Lefty," but he was really right-handed. As a young boy, he broke his right arm falling down while skating. He suffered a bad break in one of his arm bones, and for two months he resorted to doing everything left-handed. His playmates began to call him "Lefty," and, well, the nickname just stuck.

He had been wearing those skates with clamps that you adjusted with a key until they clamped tightly onto your regular shoes. Seems one of the clamps worked itself loose, causing him to trip and take a nasty spill on the concrete. They probably don't even make that cheap kind of skate anymore, but there are a lot of "Leftys" still around.

Perhaps that unfortunate childhood accident set a pattern for the rest of his life. For many years he kept trying to skate through life, but invariably, the constitutional clamps that held him up would come loose, and once again he would fall. As a person gets older, falls are harder to sustain. It was exactly that way for David "Lefty" McPherson.

Lefty was 51, a short-order cook at a pancake house, and home was a walk-up two-room efficiency apartment where the rent was as low as his self-esteem. He lived alone, his wife and child having left him 20 years earlier, when he was much stronger as well as much weaker, at least to the temptations he couldn't resist. His ex-wife found and fell in love with someone else, while Lefty just got lost and fell in love with alcohol. In fact, he was only three weeks out of the county hospital for his ongoing alcohol problem. Watching him struggle behind the counter as he hustled from one order to the next trying to keep up, many people might have written him off as just another loser, but that would have been a mistake. Fate was soon to give Lefty one more chance to get it right.

That evening after work, he fought the flight of stairs up to his apartment, showered and then sat down to read the newspaper. The bald 50-watt bulb in the shadeless lamp glared. Glancing across the front page of the newspaper, he noticed a human-interest article that immediately riveted his attention. It was a story about a fine young man in dire need of a kidney transplant and the difficulties the hospital had encountered in trying to find a compatible donor for him. The more Lefty read, the more he was touched and moved, especially by the mother's plea for assistance. Lefty felt extremely confident that the woman's son would find a compatible donor. He should have. He recognized *his* son's picture in the paper.

The next morning he called the hospital and told them of his desire to have one of his kidneys removed and given to his son. He explained about the divorce and all, and only requested one thing—that he remain anonymous. He was asked to come in for the appropriate tests the following day and was told the family would be informed of the fact that there was a potential donor, and nothing else. That night David "Lefty" McPherson slept with a clear mind and a peace that passed over him.

One week later, he was at the hospital having a kidney removed while a surgical team stood by in the adjoining suite. The hospital had kept its word and his anonymity. The transplant was a success. Later, a mother and son rejoiced on one floor of the hospital while Lefty did the same on another. He had set things right. He had atoned for his past. He had even surrendered his ego, seeing as how he didn't want recognition or credit for the good deed he had done.

Lefty is doing better these days. Sobriety is going good. He has never shared his secret with anyone—and neither has the hospital. Of course, the hospital's secret is somewhat different.

There was no doubt that Lefty was a compatible donor; all the tests were perfect matches. There also was no doubt that he was a generous and brave man. However, there was a huge doubt that he was the boy's real father. A red flag went up when Lefty told the hospital that his son was born in North Carolina. It seems their records indicated the young man was born in Tennessee. An investigation of the facts they had gathered led the hospital to conclude that although there was a remarkable physical resemblance between them, and the blood and tissue samples were perfect matches, the donor and recipient were not related. The young man was not his son after all.

Some people might explain it away by saying Lefty's years of drinking had affected his mind and he saw what he wanted to see in the newspaper, a mere figment of his imagination. Other people might say it was nothing but blind luck. The medical people attributed it to a statistical anomaly, a rare event comparable to the odds of winning a lottery.

It appears a much less rare event occurred the same day David "Lefty" McPherson left the hospital after being discharged. He was so distracted by his happiness that he failed to notice the flashing marquee in front of the nearby church as he drove by heading home. It read: "A coincidence is a small miracle where God prefers to remain anonymous." It was probably just a coincidence that he failed to see it.

5

It's About Time

To hazard much to get much has more
of avarice than wisdom.

William Penn

After 20 minutes of talking, I had a general idea of what the well-dressed man's problem was. He was having insomnia as well as high blood pressure and anxiety. His physician was concerned that the man was using alcohol to combat stress and strain, and had referred him to me.

The man was evidently successful. He embodied such terms as striver, go-getter, achievement-oriented, self-starter and money-motivated. He sat in the chair jingling his car keys with the Volvo emblem on them. I was afraid he might do irreparable damage to his Rolex watch if he didn't stop. Finally, he put the keys in his pocket and asked what I thought his problem was.

"Let me tell you a brief story I once heard," I offered, "and then tell me what it means to you."

"Okay," he answered, glancing at his watch as though he were going to time me.

"In ancient China, the emperor proclaimed a special day once a year," I began. "The whole kingdom looked forward to this day. You see, on this day, the emperor drew a name from the tax rolls, and that lucky individual had a chance to acquire land." The man leaned forward in his chair as I continued.

"The ground rules were simple. The chosen individual would begin running at sunrise and had to stop when the sun was directly overhead at noon. He had to run in a circle and finish at the same place from which he had started before high noon. If he failed to complete the circle, he didn't get any land, but if he did, he got all the land he had encircled or run around."

The man in my office glanced at his watch once again. "Is this going to be a long story?" he inquired.

"No," I assured him, "it won't take much longer." He nodded, and I continued.

"The man chosen one year by the emperor was very poor, but he was a great runner. The big day came. The man started at the place chosen by the emperor, who set his sundial on the starting line. At first the runner paced himself, but the shouts of the crowd inspired him so much that he began to run faster and in a much wider circle than he had planned. He told himself that next to the emperor, he would own more land than anyone in the entire kingdom. He would be rich."

The man in my office fidgeted, but I went on. "The man had run a great distance, and half of his tremendous circle had been completed when he noticed the sun. He had run too wide, and now he began to run faster as the sun rose in the sky. He didn't have time to stop for water and rest as he had planned. The finish line was too far away, and he might lose everything. He had to complete the circle."

The man in my office had taken his car keys out of his pocket and was jiggling them as I continued. "The emperor stood at the finish line with the sundial as the man pushed himself to run faster than he ever thought possible. Struggling, sweating and gasping for air, he sped across the finish line just seconds before the emperor signaled that the time was up. It was the most land any subject had ever won, and he had become a very rich man. Stooped over, he turned around and began to approach the emperor. Suddenly, he stopped. A terrible pain hit the runner, who grabbed his chest and fell dead at the emperor's feet."

I looked over at the man and asked, "What does this story mean to you?"

"The runner should have been a better time manager," he said without a smile. "Speaking of time," he said, glancing at his watch and rising, "I've got to go. I've got another appointment in a few minutes."

Somehow, I think this man's story won't have a happy ending either.

6

The Great Escape

An aged man is but a paltry thing,
A tattered coat upon a stick, unless
Soul clap its hands and sing, and louder sing
For every tatter in its mortal dress.

William Butler Yeats

The two old men sat on the park bench basking in the autumn sun. Sal Lorino and Lou Matsen snickered like a pair of teenagers. They had escaped in broad daylight.

"The nursing home folks won't even know we've gone until bed check tonight," Sal said, with a sparkle in his fading brown eyes.

"Yeah," Lou confirmed, "and by then we'll be miles away from here."

"Where are we going?" Sal asked.

"I ain't figured it out yet, Sal, but I'll have a plan by nightfall," Lou said, as he tapped his bald head with his finger. "Maybe Vegas."

A young man walked by and glared at them, then kept going. "Hey, Lou, why do these kids all wear their baseball caps backwards?" Sal asked.

"They all want to be catchers on their baseball teams," Lou informed him with an air of authority.

"Well, that sure is good news. Nobody wanted to be a catcher when I was a kid. We were afraid the batter would knock our brains out with the bat," Sal said, watching the young man walking out of sight.

"Well, times have changed, Sal. You've got to keep up with what's going on, or change will pass you by. What would you do without me?" Lou asked.

"I guess I'd talk to myself more than I already do. Sometimes I think I'm getting senile, Lou. What do you think?"

"I think you worry too much, Sal. You just wait till we

get to Vegas and see those showgirls. I'm telling you, they'll make your teeth fall out."

Sal put his hand to his mouth. "Oh, no, Lou, I left my teeth back at the nursing home. How am I going to eat?"

"You can use mine, I guess," Lou laughed, "but we'll have to eat in shifts."

"I ain't using your teeth, Lou. I've been your roommate for 11 years, but I draw the line at that."

"Suit yourself, you old geezer. You can eat strained peas for all I care," Lou said, as he chomped his teeth together. "I guess they have stuff like that in Las Vegas."

"Maybe I should sneak back and get my teeth," Sal said. "They probably wouldn't catch me."

Lou shook his head. "Oh, yes they would. And then they'd call your children, and it would be a mess. Knowing you, you'd probably blame it on me, and my children would try to have me committed or something. Next thing you know, we'd be eating Haldol for breakfast. I tell you what. We'll just get you a new set when we get to Vegas."

Sal thought for a moment, then said, "Okay, Lou, but I want them snow white like the movie stars."

"It's as good as done," Lou answered, and Sal smiled a toothless grin. "I'll get you a pair of certified Hollywood teeth as a souvenir of our running away together."

"Did you ever run away before, Lou?" Sal asked. "I mean ever?"

"Well, once when I was a kid I did, but I was home before dark. Never been on the lam from the nursing home. This is my very first time. How about you?"

"Nah. I've always been too afraid to run away. Never wanted to cause any trouble. I always did as I was told," Sal said.

"Well, it's about time we broke some rules, my friend.

You ain't got many years left, you know."

"Yeah, I know," Sal sighed. "Hey Lou, do you hear that thunder?"

"That ain't thunder, Sal. That's just a car going by with the bass blaring away. Don't you know anything?"

"Yeah, I know I'm getting hungry and I ain't got my teeth. And soon I'll be chilly, and I don't have my coat. That's some things I know!" Sal complained.

Lou punched Sal on the shoulder with his finger and said, "Next thing you know, you'll be telling me you like that slop over at the home and you're going to miss your baby bed with the rails on the side."

Sal punched him back. "Well, just maybe I will, Mr. Smarty Pants. It ain't all that bad, you know. The best food in the world won't do me any good if I can't chew it."

"Just stop it, Sal," Lou demanded. "I've got all my credit cards right here in my billfold." He reached into his back pocket and pulled out his wallet. "We can get whatever we want with these!"

Sal examined the credit cards in their plastic compart-ments. "My goodness, Lou, these are all gasoline credit cards. We don't even have a car. What good will they do us?"

Lou stared at the cards. "I can't believe it," he said. "The kids must have taken them. Probably thought I'd never need them at the nursing home. They should have told me. I had a right to know, don't you think?"

"I think we won't be going anywhere, Lou, unless we steal a car, eat gasoline station food, and sell the car when we get to Vegas so we can have money to gamble and see the showgirls," Sal answered.

"You're right, Sal. Maybe we should have thought this through better. Okay, maybe we should wait and run

away next year. Are you ready to walk back to the nursing home?" Lou asked, with a frown on his face.

"Last one back has to drink the other's prune juice at
supper!" Sal said as they stood for their stroll back. "Is it
a deal?"

"It's a deal," Lou said, "but no running. I've still got
my bedroom slippers on." He looked down at his feet
with a silly smile.

On their way back they passed a convenience store
on the corner where a young woman was fueling up her
new Cadillac.

"Ain't she pretty?" Lou asked, punching Sal on the
shoulder.

"She's young enough to be your great-granddaughter,
you old pervert!" Sal blustered.

"I mean the car, you old coot," Lou said.

"Well, why didn't you say so?" Sal chided.

- "I thought you were smart enough to know there ain't
nothing as pretty as a black Cadillac," Lou said, shaking
his head.

The young woman looked over at them and smiled.
They stood there, harmless-looking like the great-
grandfathers they were. She waved as she went inside
to pay for the gas.

Three weeks later, Sal and Lou were picked up by
the police in Las Vegas, Nevada. The detectives had no
trouble following the trail of the gasoline credit cards. By
then, they had sold the car and gambled away every last
penny at the fancy casino that had put them up, thinking
they were a couple of eccentric high-rolling gamblers.

The district attorney decided it would do him no good
to prosecute. He felt it would be impossible to get a
conviction, especially after seeing and talking with Lou.

Lou told him, "You see, copper, I had this planned all

along. I want you to put us in the big house and throw away the key. Let the state pay the $47,000 a year apiece it will cost them to house us. We'll get free room and board, and medicine, and our own TV. That will be great!"

The attorney sat there with an open mouth as Lou continued. "Just think of the money we'll be saving our children. We're guilty, and I beg you to convict us so we can change prisons at a substantial savings."

The attorney knew no jury was going to return a guilty verdict for two old men who each looked like Clarence, the angel in *It's a Wonderful Life*. And even if they did, the cost to the state in money and negative publicity would lead to a crucifixion by the local papers, if not the national media. He decided to call their children.

The children came up with the money for the stolen car, and the case was dropped. Sal and Lou were given a stern warning that it better never happen again. They were taken back to the nursing home, sitting obediently in the backseat as loud, angry voices came from the front about the embarrassment they had caused.

The nursing home staff was as unhappy as Sal's and Lou's children with what they had done. In contrast, the eyes of all the other patients lit up as Sal and Lou told them about their exciting adventures. Lou would always end his retelling of the story with a bad Edward G. Robinson impression as he said, "Next time we break out of this joint we're taking you with us, see." That brought laughter and smiles to those who listened and longed for one more last hurrah for themselves.

Nowadays, Sal and Lou just sit on the front porch of the nursing home and wave at the cars passing on the avenue. Sal is especially handsome, as he flashes his Hollywood teeth at every black Cadillac that passes, reminding him of *the great escape*.

7

The Cap

No one feels as light as when he is lifted up in spirit by another.

Anonymous

I always thought cigars had a unique smell. The smoke has a distinct odor, much different from that of a pipe or cigarette.

Entering a local restaurant the other day, I passed a man who was heading out, and the pungent odor of his freshly lit cigar awakened a memory connected to my sense of smell. Whoever it was that said the strongest memories are connected to smell was right. As I walked through the dense smoke, I expected to see Mr. Joseph emerge on the other side.

I found an empty table as the smell of the cigar and memories of Mr. Joseph lingered. My, how he loved his cigars. He was a short, heavy man with an easy laugh, who loved sports and young people. Mr. Joseph was a "bird dog" scout for the New York Yankees, whose duties included "sniffing out" and "pointing to" prospective talents for the Yankees' full-time scouts. Mr. Joseph wasn't full-time, mind you, just sort of a part-time scout. He sold insurance full-time.

He always wore his Yankee cap to our ball games. We knew it was a great cap because it had nine rows of stitches on the bill of it. Mr. Joseph said you could tell the quality of a baseball cap by counting the rows of stitches, with the finer caps having more. The floppy bills of our youth baseball caps only had five rows, so we knew for sure he must be right.

Mr. Joseph was the most ubiquitous man I ever knew. He seemed to be everywhere. When we played youth baseball, well, there was Mr. Joseph sitting on the first-base side in his little fold-up chair, down near the right-field foul line. When my father took me to the grown-ups' Industrial League games, there was Mr. Joseph, smoking his cigar and intently watching the game from his favorite location. He was a fixture at all the games and seemed synonymous with baseball.

We gathered around him to listen as he talked to us about baseball. I loved those times, and as we grew older, we grew closer to him. I was enthralled listening to him tell about the grand old game, weaving his stories about Ruth, Gehrig, Mantle and Berra on his loom of laughter and knowledge until we could actually see Yankee Stadium spread before us like a brilliant tapestry. Yankee Stadium became our "field of dreams" long before the movie of that name.

Mr. Joseph watched me play baseball and grow up, and after high school graduation, I was signed by a professional baseball team and assigned to a minor league team. In reality, I was probably a good pitcher but maybe not good enough to make it all the way to the major leagues. An injury to my pitching arm in my third year saved me from having to face the awful truth that perhaps I never would have made it to the big leagues. In spring training of the following year, I was released.

Unable to throw, I knew the release was coming, but like the expectation of the impending death of a loved one, it still didn't ease the pain. I packed my clothes and shattered dreams for the drive back home. Self-pity rode most of the way with me, and it was dusk as I entered the city limits.

Seeking solace, I sought my father, but as was often the case, he wasn't at his house. After he and Mother divorced, he ran head-on into his alcoholism, and it seemed to have totaled out his soul. I made the rounds of his favorite beer joints until I found him. He was well on his way to being drunk and practicing his personal philosophy of cheap women and expensive whiskey. I was too young and ignorant to know about alcoholism, but I was old enough to know he had some kind of soul sickness.

He was startled to see me, knowing I was supposed to be in spring training. He thought I had quit the team, and it took a lot of explaining to cut through his alcohol haze and make the point that I had been released because of my arm injury. Suddenly, his eyes filled with anger as he accused me of faking the injury so I could return home. I guess he was mad at me because I wasn't his professional baseball-playing son any longer, and I had cost him his bragging rights among his drinking buddies. I knew he was failing in his struggle against alcohol, but I also knew I had failed the one person whose approval I had sought my entire life.

I left and drove down 10th Avenue North. The lights from the industrial baseball field could be seen in the distance, and I turned down the side street leading to the ball diamond. I arrived, pushed the now heavy car door open, got out and walked over to the first-base side. The humidity was as high as my spirits were low.

Looking down the right-field line, the first thing I saw was the cloud of cigar smoke hanging lifeless in the air as it reflected the light and hovered above the man in the chair. It had to be him. I walked toward the smoke, but the closer I got, the more I realized it couldn't be him. This man was way too thin. Then I saw the cap with "NY" on it. It *was* Mr. Joseph, but he looked so drawn and sickly.

When he saw me coming, he pulled off his Yankees cap and gave me a playful slap on my shoulder with it.

"Hey, Big John," he said, smiling, "why aren't you in spring training? What are you doing home?"

Well, that was all it took. I told him everything—about the arm injury, the release, the ride home and the earlier conversation with my father. A left-handed batter pulled a line-drive foul. It couldn't have missed us by more than 10 feet, but Mr. Joseph didn't take his eyes off my face.

When I finished telling him everything, he sat there puffing on his cigar. Finally, his eyes looked away for a moment as he cleared his throat. Then he looked back at me.

"Boy, I know you love baseball," he said in a hoarse voice. "I sure am sorry about your arm." He hesitated, then in a stronger, more emphatic manner he said, "I've seen a lot of ball players in my day, and you're one of the finest I ever saw. You'd have been a big leaguer for sure. You had what it took!" Mr. Joseph's words made me smile, and he smiled also. Good old Mr. Joseph. He wasn't too weak to try to lift my spirits.

"But," he went on, "baseball isn't everything, you know. John, I think you'll be just fine at whatever you do. You're a natural-born winner, kid. You'll see." He started coughing. It sounded terrible and took him an awful long time to make it stop. I was uneasy and tried to make conversation to ease my awkwardness.

"You still have your Yankees cap," I said, pointing toward it. "How long have you had it?"

"Too long," he replied, as he gently took it from his head and stared at it in his hands. "You know what, kid? I'm tired of this cap. Here, you take it. I think I'll get me a new one."

"Do you really mean it?" I asked.

"Sure I do," he answered, as he placed it on my head. "See, it's a perfect fit."

Mr. Joseph St. Clair never went to another baseball game, and later on that summer he died from the ravages of lung cancer.

Once, after his funeral, I overheard some men saying that Mr. Joseph never was a "real" baseball scout. One of the men said he doubted whether the Yankees cap he always wore was authentic. I guess the truth is, I never cared what they said. All I know is that whenever I look down the right-field line of any ballpark, I expect to see Mr. Joseph with his cigar smoke rising out from under his Yankees cap.

No, I didn't believe any of the negative comments about him that followed his death. You see, I know something about Mr. Joseph that perhaps no one else on earth knows. That night, so long ago, as I sat in the damp grass along the right-field foul line, I was in the presence of crickets and a guardian angel. I'm convinced Mr. Joseph got his new cap all right, and I just bet you it was a halo.

8

The Richest Man in Town?

When we do the best we can, we never know what miracle is wrought in our life, or the life of another.

Helen Keller

Mr. Oscar Henderson was a rich man. He owned Henderson Hardware, Henderson Department Store, Henderson Drugs and Sundries, and one of the local car dealerships, which not surprisingly was called Henderson Motors. He was a huge man whose waist had grown right along with his businesses. He loved the Christmas season because that was when money flowed into his bank accounts like a swollen river flood. Mr. Henderson never could get enough money, it seemed. It was as if he had been born with this cavernous craving for money, and enough was never enough. His smiles grew broader as the December days passed.

Charles Simpson was the kind of man used to *not* having the word "Mister" as part of his name. "Charlie" was pretty much what people called him whenever they chose to speak to him. He never could get enough money either, it seemed, but then this was common for a drifter like Charlie. He was slim and bent, like a pine tree that had grown up beside giant oaks that had hidden it from the sun and sucked the nutrients from the surrounding soil. Charlie had no way of knowing that when he jumped down from the boxcar of the train he had ridden in on, he would be landing in the shadow of such a giant oak as Mr. Oscar Henderson. The only thing Charlie Simpson and Mr. Oscar Henderson had in common was that they both loved Christmas, but for different reasons.

Charlie got a cheap room, cleaned up, put on his best clothes (corduroy pants and a plaid shirt), bought a paper for the want ads and applied for the listed job as Santa at the Henderson Department Store. Circumstance smiled at Charlie, who in turn smiled at the personnel manager when he said Charlie was hired and could start work on Monday, with a fake beard and appropriate padding, of course. So it began.

Each day from nine to five, the children came and sat on Charlie's lap. Sometimes they'd have their pictures taken, but most of the time they'd just tell him what they wanted for Christmas. Charlie gave them each a genuine laugh and told them he'd do the best he could, though he had to admit that some of the children's lists were so long he couldn't believe it was just for one child.

One day, near closing time, Charlie noticed a little boy standing in line by himself. The little tyke appeared to be six or seven, was shabbily dressed and carried a piece of newspaper. The boy's appearance tugged at Charlie's heart, but when he saw the boy limping toward him with one leg shorter than the other, it was like a tugboat was pulling on it.

Charlie hoisted him up to his lap and asked, "Well, well, what is your name little boy, and what do you want Santa to bring you for Christmas?"

"You didn't ask me if I'd been a good boy this year, Santa!" the youngster said.

"That's right, I didn't," Charlie replied. "Well, tell me then, have you been a good boy this year?"

"No, I haven't, Santa! My name is Johnny Barlow, and I live at 1231 Third Court South. And I have been bad, real bad—so bad I don't deserve nothing this year." The reply startled Charlie, who sat there open-mouthed.

The boy continued before Charlie could regain his composure. "So, I don't deserve stuff Santa, and I don't want it anyway. What I do want," he said, opening the newspaper, "is for you to take whatever you was going to give me if I hadda been good and trade it in on this stuff for my family."

Charlie looked at the newspaper. The boy was pointing at the ad for the Super-Saver Grocery Store, which had pictures of the food items listed as well as their sale prices. "By 'stuff,' you mean this food here?" Charlie asked, as he pointed at the pictures of the food.

"Yes sir, that's what I want you to give my family. Momma says we're in a bad way, and we need for Santa to bring us some food so my younger brothers and sisters can have something to put in their stomachs."

Charlie was at a loss for words. He had seen grown men jobless and hungry, but they could fend for themselves. This little boy with a limp—well, it just didn't seem fair at all.

"Okay," Charlie said, "I guess I'll do what you say!" This brought a smile to Johnny's face as Charlie continued, "Now, run along home." As soon as the words came out of his mouth, Charlie could have bit his tongue off. "I mean, go on home and tell your family that Santa is bringing good stuff for Christmas." He watched as the young boy limped off and left the store. Charlie said the address over and over in his mind as he went to put on his street clothes.

While changing clothes in the employee dressing room, he asked Mr. Dunwoody, one of the salesmen, "Who is the richest man in this town?" Mr. Dunwoody looked at Charlie as though he had just asked the salesman what country they were in. Then Mr. Dunwoody replied, "Why, Mr. Oscar Henderson!"

"Thank you," Charlie said, and finished dressing. He now knew what he had to do. Christmas was only three days away.

At nine o'clock that night, Charlie Simpson knocked on the huge oak front door of Mr. Oscar Henderson's mansion. A butler opened the door and inquired as to Charlie's name and the nature of his business.

"Please tell Mr. Henderson that my name is Charlie Simpson and that I work as a Santa at his department store, and it is urgent, maybe even a matter of life or death, that I see him." The butler's chin rose up high in the air, but he turned to deliver the message as he had been told.

It took a while, but he returned with a terse message that "Mr. Henderson will see you for five minutes if it's that important."

"It is," Charlie responded, and followed the dignified butler back to Mr. Henderson's study.

Charlie told Mr. Henderson, as quickly as he could, all about the boy named Johnny Barlow, but Mr. Henderson was unmoved by his words. He then pleaded with Mr. Henderson, but Mr. Henderson had no desire to donate any money to help the family. Soon, Mr. Henderson rudely cut Charlie off by saying, "Your time is up. Malcolm will see you out!" He summoned Malcolm to escort Charlie to the door.

Malcolm led Charlie back to the front door. Looking over his shoulder to make sure Mr. Henderson was still back in the study, the butler stepped out onto the front porch and shut the door. "Mr. Simpson," he said, "my name is Malcolm T. Morgan, and I have been the butler here for three years. I overheard your conversation with Mr. Henderson. It is a kind thing you want to do, and I desire to help you in your endeavor." Malcolm's chin was no longer in the air, but on his chest as he said, "I'm sorry I'm so well trained at being snooty. Please forgive me if I offended you. Now, let me help you. How much money do you think you'll need for this boy and his family?"

"A hundred would really help, but anything you could spare would be most appreciated," Charlie said. "It sure is mighty nice of you, Malcolm, to do this."

Malcolm pulled out his checkbook and pen from his breast pocket, moved over under the globe light on the porch and scribbled out a check, which he then handed to Charlie. Charlie, not wanting to appear rude, placed it in his shirt pocket without looking at the amount.

"I don't understand men like Henderson," Charlie said, "but I imagine someday he will get his."

Malcolm's chin rose until he was staring right down his nose at Charlie. "I'll have you to understand, Mr. Simpson, that I have been a professional butler my entire life, serving in England as well as here in the United States. In my time, I have worked for many a bitter widow and quite a few eccentric misers, and I've done so for purely selfish reasons. You see, Mr. Simpson, you are wrong. Mr. Henderson will never get his. *I will get his*, just like the other fortunes I have inherited during my time. I imagine I have become quite wealthy in my own right over the years."

Then, dropping his chin once again and smiling at their secret, Malcolm said, "Run along, Mr. Simpson. You are a good man in God's service. Merry Christmas to you and to young Johnny."

Well, that was the Christmas season that Mrs. Barlow bought her children several months of groceries, and toys and clothes for them all. Johnny Barlow was fitted for a special orthopedic shoe so he could walk without a limp, and he was taken to the doctor in Mrs. Barlow's new car. Mrs. Barlow opened her very first checking account at the First National Bank.

It was wonderful to see how surprised and happy the Barlows were. But not a one of them was as surprised as Charlie Simpson was when he got back to his cheap hotel room that night after going to Mr. Henderson's house, and opened the check to see it was made out to Johnny Barlow in the amount of one hundred *thousand* dollars. Charlie really had gone to see the richest man in town—he just hadn't known it at the time.

9

Two Hearts Harvey

It is the heart which experiences God, and not reason.

Blaise Pascal

Harvey Patterson lived in the same neighborhood as my Grandma Allen. When Harvey was just a young boy he got very sick, and his temperature soared so high that for several days the doctors wondered whether he was going to live. Finally, the fever broke, but he was left with brain damage that gave him the mind of a child forever. His mouth twisted to the side when he talked, and although he wasn't very smart, he was aware enough of this defect to be embarrassed. He was in his 30s when I first met him, during my last year in high school, when I went to live with Grandma Allen after my parents had gone their separate ways. However, Grandma had known him his whole life, even before the fiery fever that had burned down his brain. She said she liked Harvey Patterson, seeing as how he was a child of God. She said the fever may have left him with just half a brain but that God had given him a heart twice as big as anybody else's, and that was the most special gift any-one could have. She told me if she ever heard me say anything bad about him, she'd wash my mouth out with Octagon soap, and she was a woman of such conviction that I knew for sure she had told me the gospel truth.

Harvey Patterson only came by Grandma Allen's on Sundays. The other six days he worked two jobs and never got home before dark. He was a carpenter's helper during the day, a job my Granddaddy Allen had found for him before cancer chewed away Granddaddy's life. Harvey also was a grocery sacker and loader at the local supermarket in the evenings and on Saturdays.

Whatever people may have said about him, no one could say he was lazy. Sunday came, and so did Harvey.

Grandma was shelling peas, shucking corn and helping me peel away the skin of my ripening dreams when the dogs in the neighborhood started barking. She just sat there in her rocker on the front porch and, without looking, said, "That must be Harvey coming. Those dogs only bark that way when Harvey or the dog catcher is around, and I know the dog catcher doesn't work on Sunday." She was right, as he came up the street with a dozen or so dogs dancing around him as only dogs can do when they're happy to see someone. He had a big brown grocery sack and was giving out something to the dogs.

"What's he got in that sack, Grandma?" I asked, as she continued shelling the peas.

"Bones and fat trimmings that the butcher gives him over at the grocery store where he works," she said. "I wouldn't be surprised if those dogs don't curl up every Saturday night dreaming about him coming every Sunday." She smiled and set the pan of peas down. By the time Harvey got to our porch he had doled out all of his dog's dreams from his sack, and each dog was in his own little world, gnawing away and probably thinking of good hiding places for the bones. Grandma spoke first.

"Harvey, those dogs wait and watch for you like a widow woman does the mailman bringing her Social Security check," she chuckled. Harvey smiled a lopsided grin as he folded the stained sack and placed it in his back pocket.

"I love those dogs, Mrs. Allen," he said from the side of his mouth, as his eyes darted toward me. "They all go to heaven. Ain't that the truth, Mrs. Allen?"

Grandma gave him a knowing nod. "That's the truth,

Harvey," she said. "I suppose God sprinkles their souls with brown sugar when they're born and they just get sweeter every day."

Harvey laughed out loud. He started to put his hand up to his face, then stopped. "I almost forgot, Mrs. Allen. You said I should never be ashamed of how I look 'cause you see God's face in me."

"I sure do," Grandma Allen said with that conviction of hers. "Sure as it's Sunday, I do. Why, Harvey, even those dogs know that's the truth. Come up here on the porch. I want you to meet my grandson, Johnny!"

He lumbered up the steps and opened the screen door. His grip was like a leathery vise when I shook his hand. Grandma beckoned him to sit in one of the rockers. Then she went into the house and came back out with a plate of fudge. He and I cleaned that plate except for one piece Grandma Allen got for herself. She said she "had seen hungry hogs eat slower." Harvey and I laughed. Grandma loved to see kids eat her fudge until they looked like old men with tobacco juice in the corners of their mouths. I suppose that's the way we looked because she made us go down to the water hydrant beside the front steps and wash off our faces. We used our sleeves as towels. Harvey and I talked about dogs, and baseball, and how hard it was to sack groceries and make sure the right items went into the right sacks.

Grandma listened to us as she shelled and shucked with a huge smile on her lips. Grandma Allen made it seem as though heaven were right there on that screened-in front porch with the wooden floors. It was as if we were the first two angels she had met and she wanted to hear all about us. It was a grand afternoon. Finally, she finished her task and sat in her rocker, with both hands holding the ends of the wooden arms as she gently swayed back and forth. "If you two boys will take this corn and peas into the kitchen, I might tell you a story when you come back," she said with gleaming eyes. We were back before our own rockers had quit moving, and once the rhythm of our rockers matched hers, she began.

"Once upon a time there were two brothers. They ran and played and laughed until their mother tucked them in their beds at night. One night an evil spirit came into the boys' bedroom while they dreamed their dreams. The oldest boy always slept next to the window to protect his younger brother in case a huge robber tried to come through the screen on those hot nights when the window was open. But that night, the evil spirit had turned itself into a robber so small that it was no bigger than a piece of dust. Still, the older brother saw him and swallowed him up before he could make it over to the younger boy, who was asleep in the nearby bed. That night the tiny robber stole some of the older brother's ability to think. But since the boy had prayed before going to sleep that night, God saw this and decided to give him a double helping of heart and love to make up for what had been taken." Grandma Allen was of Cherokee Indian heritage, and her proud face glowed, reflecting the setting sun, as she continued.

"In the Cherokee tribe, the older brother would have been called 'Two Hearts,' and that will be his name from now on in this story," she said, as she held two fingers up in the evening air.

"So, Two Hearts grew up with God on his face and the spirit of angels in his breast. Sometimes humans can't see these things, but dogs and little children who are never blind to these things can't be fooled, and they loved Two Hearts and followed him everywhere he went. Two Hearts watered the flowers with his kisses and danced to drums that only he could hear. He spoke to angels that only he could see, and their wings dried his hot tears when people made fun of him." Grandma adjusted her spectacles, and I glanced at Harvey, who was nodding his head in agreement with Grandma's words. She continued.

"Two Hearts was such a wonderful young boy that God decided to make him a guardian angel for his younger brother, who, as he grew up, longed to become a doctor. The family was poor, but Two Hearts worked two jobs so he could help send his brother to college and medical school. Never once did he complain. The only letters he had ever sent in his entire life were those containing the money orders he mailed to the schools. Two Hearts had sworn to God he would always keep it a secret about his being a guardian angel, and the younger brother never knew who his benefactor was."

Harvey raised his hand like a schoolchild. "What is it, Harvey?" Grandma Allen asked in a sweet tone.

"What does *benefactor* mean?" he asked as he tilted his head to one side.

"A benefactor is some person who does good," she answered, and he straightened his head and smiled.

"So," Grandma went on, "every day, before the sun rises, God and His angels sit around drinking coffee and praising the goodness of the man with two hearts. One day God started to speak, and the angels fell silent, just like they always do when He speaks. God looked at the angels and asked, 'Don't you think Two Hearts is look-ing more like me as the years go by?' All the angels spoke as one: 'Oh, yes, he is becoming the spitting image of you, Lord!' 'I thought so,' said the Lord, as He glanced down for one more look at His wonderful child,

Two Hearts, before pulling the sun up in the eastern sky."

Grandma said, "The end," and Harvey clapped like crazy and kept saying, "That's so good, Mrs. Allen, that's so good! That's the best story I ever heard!"

"Thank you, Harvey," Grandma Allen said. "Coming from you, I do believe that's the best compliment I ever got."

Harvey stood up. "I have to go," he said. "I want to go home and tell my dog that story before he goes to sleep. Nice to meet you, Johnny."

"Thank you for coming by, Harvey," Grandma's sincere voice rang out. "You take care of yourself!"

Harvey walked off down the sidewalk, being careful not to step on any of the cracks. When he got to the end of the block, he turned and waved good-bye. I returned the gesture. I looked over at Grandma, who had taken off her spectacles and was dabbing the corners of her eyes with the edge of her apron. I thought maybe some gnats had landed in her eyes.

"That was a wonderful story, Grandma Allen," I said. "You made it sound so real."

"It was," she replied, as it finally dawned on me she had tears in her eyes.

"But why are you crying?" I asked her. "The ending was beautiful and happy, not sad."

She finished drying her eyes, then put her spectacles back in place before she answered. "Sometimes it just overwhelms me when I see the face of God," she said.

Suddenly I began to cry. For the first time in my life, I realized what was so special about Grandma Allen. I was looking at the face of God in her.

10

Reflections

... but the tongue can no man tame; it
is an unruly evil, full of deadly poison.

James 3:8

"I'm telling you, Joan Benson is the most stuck-up woman I ever saw," Mrs. Tyler said, dusting off the merchandise in her women's clothing shop. "Always looking at herself in the shop window reflection as she passes by. Why, one day she was in trying on clothes and she rubbed her face in the mirror. I mean, not her face, mind you, but the reflection in the mirror. Can you beat that?" she asked with a smirk on her face.

"I've seen her do that, too," Mrs. Childs, her employee, answered, rolling her eyes back up into her head. "But I think she's more stuck on herself than stuck-up. She's always been nice to me, although she's only been in town for about six months." Mrs. Tyler didn't like Mrs. Childs's last words because the compliment cut her gossip short, and she just loved to gossip about other people. "Well, nice or not, she's strange, I tell you, mighty, mighty strange. Look! Speaking of the devil, here she comes now."

Miss Joan Benson stopped and stood in front of the store window. Sure enough, in a few moments it was obvious she was staring at her reflection. She smiled a beautiful smile as her teeth caught the sun, making them snowy white. She was gorgeous for sure. Slowly, she began to trace her reflection with her fingers pressed against the glass.

"See, I told you she was strange!" Mrs. Tyler exclaimed. "Not only is she egotistical, she's messing up my window. Get that Windex and get out there and clean her fingerprints off the window, Mrs. Childs."

"You mean right now?" Mrs. Childs inquired.

"Yes, right this minute!" Mrs. Tyler answered in a huff. "It'll serve her right if it embarrasses her. Hurry before she has a chance to leave or come inside."

Mrs. Childs got the glass cleaner and some paper towels from beneath the counter and rushed outside. She knew better than to cross Mrs. Tyler, who had a reputation for destroying many people's characters with a well-placed rumor and vicious gossip.

She knew Mrs. Tyler was watching, so Mrs. Childs stepped right in front of Joan Benson and sprayed the window.

"Good morning, Mrs. Childs," Miss Benson said in a soft voice. "Oh, I'm sorry. I must have smeared the window. Here, let me help you," she offered, as she took a towel from the roll Mrs. Childs was holding and wiped the window.

Mrs. Childs saw Mrs. Tyler glaring from inside the store as Miss Benson rubbed the glass clean. "There, that should do it," Miss Benson said as she stepped back from the window and handed Mrs. Childs the used paper towel.

Mrs. Childs couldn't think of anything to say except "Thank you." Miss Benson looked at her image in the window one more time, waved good-bye toward the window and left.

Mrs. Childs went inside, where Mrs. Tyler was impatiently tapping her foot. "Do you think she saw me watching her?" she asked. "Was she waving at me through the window? I bet she thought she was being cute, mocking me like that. Well, what do you think?"

"I'm not sure," Mrs. Childs answered, "but I think she was waving at herself."

"Well, whether she was waving at me or herself, I

think she was being a little too smug to suit me. Don't you agree?" Mrs. Tyler's cross-examining tone matched her stern face.

Mrs. Childs could only mutter, "Yes," as she quickly busied herself straightening the stacks of blouses at a nearby table. Mrs. Childs had seen the lightning flash in Mrs. Tyler's eyes and knew a severe storm was on the horizon for the unsuspecting Joan Benson. Mrs. Childs hid beneath an umbrella of usefulness as she continued pushing the blouses around, pretending to straighten them up. Meanwhile, Mrs. Tyler was looking forward to the upcoming women's garden club meeting. She was especially interested in planting rumors.

Later that day, the garden club meeting was over, and the women milled around Mrs. Gruber's huge dining room table, munching on snacks and talking. Mrs. Gruber was a wealthy widow whose husband had owned 23 funeral homes before his death. She was the most influential woman in town, and to be invited for a sit-down dinner at her home was the equivalent of being placed in the social register. However, since her husband's death, she had done no entertaining and had become somewhat reclusive except for the monthly garden club meetings. She was a shrewd woman and spent most of her time studying investments and acquiring even more money.

"Your table is gorgeous," Mrs. Tyler's artificially sweetened voice murmured to Mrs. Gruber. "I've heard you could seat 24 people for dinner when the center leaf is pulled out. Is that true?"

"Something like that," Mrs. Gruber answered, as she stood there looking elegant in her Dior dress. "Maybe someday we old hens will have a party here and just see how many we can seat."

"Well, wouldn't that be marvelous," Mrs. Tyler said. "I imagine any woman I know but one would just love to have dinner here." The storm had started.

"Oh?" Mrs. Gruber remarked in a loud voice. "And just who might that woman be?"

The other garden club women had heard Mrs. Gruber's raised voice, and they fell silent to listen as Mrs. Tyler continued. "Oh, just one of my customers who told me she thought you were a snob, but she's a nutcase anyway. Probably didn't even know what she was saying. I really shouldn't have said anything." Mrs. Tyler looked down at the floor, waiting for her plan to work.

"Well, since you did, why don't you just continue," Mrs. Gruber demanded.

Mrs. Tyler's bait had been taken. "Well, Mrs. Childs can tell you about her. She knows how crazy the woman is. Why don't you tell her about the mirror stuff, Mrs. Childs." Mrs. Tyler had handed off the bashing baton. Mrs. Childs reluctantly began telling about this woman who was enamored with her own reflection. Mrs. Childs did a thorough job, except for telling the name, and finished with, "But she's always been nice to me."

Mrs. Gruber turned pale and sat down at the table. One of the women went to get her a wet washcloth. The blood came back to her face before the woman returned. She turned to Mrs. Tyler. "You're positive about how this woman behaves when she sees her reflection?" she asked.

"Absolutely," Mrs. Tyler answered, then added, "Sounds like *she's* the snob if you ask me."

"Is her name Joan Benson?" Mrs. Gruber questioned.

A startled Mrs. Tyler answered, "It sure is. How did you know? Did Mrs. Childs tell you?" The other women waited for the answer.

Mrs. Gruber didn't respond, but instead instructed the large group of women to pull up the chairs that encircled the huge dining room and be seated. Without the leaf, the table sat all 18 women.

"Years ago," she told her curious and attentive audience, "my husband and I opened our first funeral home in the small town of Columbia. Our first burial was a little girl named Carol Benson. She and her identical twin sister, Joan, were swimming in a pond one day, and Carol drowned. All funerals are sad, but this one was the saddest I ever saw. You see, this little girl, Joan, saw her own reflection in one of our mirrors in the hall of the funeral home and was screaming at the top of her lungs that she had found Carol, that she wasn't really dead."

Mrs. Tyler interjected, "I'm sorry. I had no way of knowing."

Mrs. Gruber ignored her and went on talking. "She must have really loved her sister and was so severely traumatized that no matter where she went, if she saw her reflection, she stopped and touched it as though it were her sister looking back at her. The whole town knew about Joan Benson's behavior and just accepted it." The women of the garden club sat still, as though they had been planted in their cherrywood seats.

"So, little Joan Benson grew up never getting over her sister. She used to come by the funeral home after school, and she would talk for hours about her twin sister, Carol. I tell you, she was the sweetest little girl I ever saw. It is so wonderful to hear she has moved to our town, and I can't wait to see her again!" The women were smiling to see Mrs. Gruber come to life.

"Ladies, we'll have a big dinner party next Thursday night to honor Miss Joan Benson," Mrs. Gruber announced to the applause of the club members. "You're all invited!"

The club women rose to leave, chattering in their excitement. Most of the women were making their way out, except for Mrs. Tyler, who just stood there, stunned. Finally, Mrs. Tyler started to leave, but she was pulled aside by Mrs. Gruber, who, with a wry smile, said, "Oh, by the way Mrs. Tyler, my table really doesn't seat *that* many people. I'm sorry, but I'm afraid I'll have to ask you not to come so our guest of honor will have a seat."

Mrs. Tyler started to protest, but Mrs. Gruber interrupted her and said, "And for your information, you're an awful liar. I'm the best liar there is, and I should know."

Then with a truly wicked grin, Mrs. Gruber said, "I know just about everything that goes on with the people in this town and for sure was aware that a Miss Joan Benson had moved here a while back. Other than that, I've never even met the woman. Yet, surely she won't be as mean-spirited as you."

Mrs. Tyler swallowed hard and left. Passing the mirror in the dining room, she saw her reflection, and it wasn't very pretty.

11

Waiting on Halley's Comet

Real friendship is shown in times of trouble; prosperity is full of friends.

Euripides

Ben was a bear of a man, a grizzly of a man, but he was no "Gentle Ben." He owned and bartended a tavern two blocks down from the pipe foundry where Uncle George worked. Uncle George, in contrast, was a small, cuddly teddy bear. In the evenings, these two polar opposite bears hibernated together inside Ben's sparsely lit tavern. It seemed appropriate since it was always winter in Uncle George's mind.

Worries fell like giant snowflakes in Uncle George's troubled brain, accumulating in drifts of desperation. A few drinks of Bacardi, however, would soon sweep the sidewalks of his mind until they were bright and clean and led to a house of glowing happiness at the end of his road of rum.

There he was, each day after work, sitting on his favorite bar stool, telling Ben the absolute answers to life, as though Ben really wanted to know. But Ben never read "Dear Abby" or even the newspaper for that matter. Ben simply couldn't read, but he could bartend, bounce and work a cash register.

In the old days, Ben was well known for his talent of snatching off beer bottle caps with his teeth. Except for this feat, which he performed nonchalantly, a person might have thought Ben was toothless since he rarely exposed his teeth by laughing. Uncle George said Ben only smiled when Halley's comet came around, but Ben didn't laugh at this of course. He knew nothing about comets, but he did know how to make someone see stars.

Ben had been a professional boxer in his younger days. His huge hands were so wide you couldn't actually see the beer cans that he slid down the bar to his customers. All boxing had done for Ben was give him a grubstake to open the bar and a genuine label as a man to be feared. His reputation would lie around like a reptile in the sun until about once or twice a year, some unfortunate man would get crazy drunk—or be just plain crazy, as Uncle George called it, and Ben would use his open hand to knock the ex-patron out cold. "Enough is enough," were Ben's sparse words. The bar took on an air as though a Supreme Court justice had ordered the deed to be done and Ben to execute the order, and no judge's courtroom was as quiet as it got in the tavern when Ben said those few words. No one doubted that Ben could actually kill a man with his bare hands—or "bear" hands, as Uncle George called them with a devilish gleam and grin, once the rum had stirred his bravado and humor.

It was clear to the patrons that Ben and Uncle George had a special relationship, but no one could really figure out why.

Uncle George was a small man with big dreams. Aunt Maggie loved him. She made no pretense that he was a blue blood. He was a blue-collar man through and through, and she had already accepted that. She had whittled her dreams down to house, food and clothes for little Jack and Jill (their names being the late Friday-night brainchild of Uncle George, who was called to the hospital from Ben's tavern the night the twins were born six years ago).

Aunt Maggie was a good woman who probably had every reason to be a bad one. Yet, Uncle George was her other "baby," and mothers are fiercely loyal to their children. So, although she may not have liked the cards that life had dealt her, she sure as hell wasn't leaving the table. She had anteed up her life.

The winds of fate blew bitter and hard in early December of 1953, rattling the shutters of Uncle George's soul. The pipe foundry had a big layoff that month, and it caught Uncle George in its trap. Teddy bears are too fragile to sustain such pain, especially when the jaws of misfortune clamp down so fast and hard. Uncle George lost his job first, and shortly after that, or so it seemed, he lost his mind. A blue-collar man without his job is not a man in his own eyes. The company's cutback had emasculated him, but without malice or purpose. It was just a fact that they were more interested in pipes and profits than in people.

My father, saved by seniority, tried to console him. But no one was able to talk sense to Uncle George as he began a rum rampage that brought out the very worst in his character.

It was sleeting outside the night Uncle George made his way to a bar stool in the tavern. The place was noisy with the Friday-night crowd from the foundry. He was half drunk when he came in that night, and it wasn't long before he was filled up to the brim and trying to keep his balance on the bar stool.

The man sitting next to Uncle George cast an innocent glance his way, but the paranoia of Uncle George's recent poverty caused him to misinterpret it. Words fueled by frustration and rum flew fast from the twisted mouth and soul of Uncle George, as the demon rum put hellfire in his eyes until they looked like black, smoldering coals. Before Ben could get there from the other end of the bar, the man had pulled and stuck a switchblade into poor Uncle George's stomach. Ben, who had a

running start, hit the knife-wielding man with his gigan-
tic fist, which ended the fight as the unconscious man
slid across the splintered floor of the tavern. Uncle
George, feeling the warmth of his own insides, leaned
forward as he screamed and lurched toward the front
door with a pitiful, panicked look in his eyes. He was
heading for home like a hurt child desperately seeking
his mother. "Maggie! Maggie!" he bellowed, as he hurled
himself through the doorway and burst across the sidewalk into the busy street, with his head down. He was a
homing pigeon in flight.

Ben had made it as far as the open doorway when he
saw the 1953 Pontiac bearing down on Uncle George.
He could only scream "No!" as the Indian on the hood
was the first part of the car to strike his friend.

The same George who for 10 years had tried in vain to
teach his friend Ben how to read, the same George who
always said Ben was his hero, the same George who
would not let Ben die on the battlefield in Italy—this
same George, this teddy bear of a man, who had carried
the severely wounded grizzly named Ben for three miles
through enemy fire rather than let Ben die in a town
whose name he couldn't pronounce, this same George
was instantly propelled up into the air by the impact, and
he came back down onto the hood with his broken body
finally coming to rest against the windshield.

The man on the floor in the tavern lived, although he
spent a week of his life in a coma. But Uncle George, he
died right there on top of that preacher's new Pontiac.
Uncle George used to joke, on those rare occasions
when Aunt Maggie could corral him into the church, that
the preacher was a lethal weapon, seeing as how he
could probably talk a man to death. Yet, it was the
preacher's car, not his words, that finally closed Uncle

George's eyes forever. The sleet and Ben's tears fell heavily onto 10th Avenue North that night.

Aunt Maggie had no life insurance or money, but she did have a burial policy. After the funeral, she found a strange comfort in knowing for certain where Uncle George would be that night for the first time in many years. There would be no more waiting up for him to stagger home, no more late suppers, and no more undressing and putting him to bed. Yet, watching her at the funeral, you knew she'd trade all her tomorrows for just one more night of lying in Uncle George's gentle arms when he was sober.

Christmas came, and so did two new Schwinn bicycles, a red one for Jack and a blue one for Jill. Jill had a strange, glowing countenance as she told us how Santa Claus had come to see her two nights before Christmas. We were true believers, so we listened closely.

Jill was asleep in the front-porch bedroom, with the window cracked open because she had a stuffy nose from a cold and couldn't breathe very well. Aunt Maggie had pried the window up with a poker, but although she had lifted all of her weight onto the poker, she only managed to lift the window several inches. Aunt Maggie then kissed Jill good-night and returned to her own bedroom, where she alternated between praying and worrying about what she was going to do for the children's Christmas, and about keeping a roof over their heads and food in their stomachs.

Jill was startled awake by the sound of heavy foot-steps coming across the porch and causing the old boards to creak. The next thing she saw was a huge hand placing two fingers in the crack beneath the stuck window and raising it with ease. She told us that Santa then put his red-sleeved arm through the window and handed her a brown paper sack. He told her to take it to her momma, wished her a Merry Christmas, then laughing a "Ho, ho, ho!" disappeared into the night. When we asked her if it was true that Santa had a long white beard, she said she never saw his face.

Aunt Maggie was kneeling by her bedside when Jill, almost sleepwalking, stumbled into the bedroom with the sack. "Here, Momma," Jill mumbled, rubbing her eyes with her free hand. "Santa said for me to give this to you."

Aunt Maggie, thinking perhaps Jill was playing some kind of trick on her, turned the bag upside down on top of the bed. Out fell what looked like a brick wrapped in white paper with the words "Mary Xmus" printed in pencil on one of the sides. Aunt Maggie gasped when she opened the "brick" to find hundreds of $20 bills neatly tied with a string. She questioned Jill, but Jill told her she had seen nothing that night but a huge hand and a red sleeve.

"Oh, Momma, I sure wish I could have seen Santa's face when he laughed," she said, as she imitated the "Ho, ho, ho!" "He must have the sweetest face in the whole world when he laughs." Jill's eyes began to flicker in sleep's Morse code as Aunt Maggie's eyes grew damp with their own message.

Aunt Maggie hugged her tightly as she carried her back to the front-porch bedroom, speaking softly to her as she slowly drifted off in her arms. "Sweet dreams," she said as she gently stroked Jill's hair. Aunt Maggie covered Jill up, putting her teddy bear next to her, as a smile covered her own face. "Someday, you'll see his laughing face, sweetheart, but I'm afraid you'll have to wait for Halley's comet to come around again."

12

Grandma's Dream

Love should be a tree whose roots are deep in the earth, but whose branches extend into heaven.

Bertrand Russell

A lot of people in psychology talk about unconditional love—when a person is loved without any conditions. In other words, no matter what that person does, the unconditional love for that person never wavers. Unfortunately, in the real world, conditions are often placed upon us, and this conditional love depends upon our meeting those expectations. Failure to meet those expectations leads to a lessening or loss of love, with the possible exception of our children, whom we seem to always love no matter what they do.

Husbands and wives very seldom have unconditional love for each other, although perhaps they should. If they did, we would have a lot fewer divorces and separations, and a sight more forgiveness. It seems very few of us can attain this elusive attribute called unconditional love.

In college, many professors tried to explain this concept of unconditional love to me, but they did so, ironically, holding a red pencil over my head like a sword. They had conditions and expectations that had to be met. If not, you were ejected from the ivory tower of graduate school. From Santa Claus to Sigmund Freud, you better be good, or else. One night when I was studying and struggling to even imagine this concept, I remembered back to a summer evening when I was sitting on the front porch with Grandma Allen.

One time, Harvey Patterson had asked her whether it was true that all dogs go to heaven. She had assured him that was the truth. That evening, I asked her about what she had said.

"Grandma, do you really think all dogs go to heaven?" I asked her. "You told Harvey they do."

"Sure they do, Johnny!" she answered, looking out at the setting sun. "That's where they come from, so, in a way, they're just going home."

"Oh, Grandma, how do you know that?" I asked with a sassy sigh.

"It came to me in a dream one night," she answered, "and it was as real as that sun in the sky."

"What was the dream about?" I asked.

"You don't tell your dreams to doubters!" she said in a stern voice, as she rocked faster.

"I'm sorry, Grandma Allen," I apologized. "I didn't mean to be a smart aleck. I mean, if you believe in something, then I do, too. Please tell me your dream," I pleaded, and her rocker slowed to a leisurely pace.

"Okay," she said. "Are you ready to listen?"

"I'm ready," I answered.

"Well, in this dream, I go to heaven, and St. Peter is standing at the pearly gates. He recognizes me and calls me by my name. I walk up to him, and he has this big smile on his face. He tells me I did a good job on earth and says he has a secret he wants to share with me. 'It is a secret that is only revealed when you cross over into heaven,' he says, and I sure am relieved to hear that good news about crossing over."

"What was the secret?" I asked with wide eyes, as Grandma Allen closed hers to focus on recalling the vision she had.

"All the dogs on earth are angels sent by God to show us His love," she said, "and we have no earthly idea of this until we get to heaven and see them with their beautiful wings, as they fly around rejoicing with all the other angels."

"You mean you saw dogs flying around heaven?" I asked.

"I sure did," she smiled. "I even saw Toni, and he was so beautiful and happy."

Toni was a stray dog that Grandma Allen had sort of adopted, and he hung around her house until one day a truck ran over him out in the street. I played with him when I was just a small boy. "You saw Toni? Did you really, Grandma?" I asked.

"I sure did!" she said, and her words made me happy in my heart.

"Did he recognize you?" I asked.

"Of course he did," she answered. "He flew down to me, and I petted him for a long time. But that wasn't even the best part."

"What do you mean, Grandma? What was the best part?" I asked, as I watched her smiling.

"Toni *talked* to me and asked how you were doing! He said he was sorry that he couldn't talk to you or me when he was on earth, but God had forbidden it when He made Toni an angel. God told him that he could only show his love through actions and not words. Toni asked me if I thought he had done a good job with you."

"What did you tell him, Grandma?" I asked, leaning forward in my rocker.

"I told him he had been a true angel. He loved you when you forgot to feed him. He came to you even after you scolded him. He waited for you to come play with him when you were off doing something else. No matter what you did, his love was always steadfast and true. That's what I told him," Grandma said.

"Did it make him happy?" I asked.

"Oh, yes," she said. "In the most beautiful voice I ever

heard, he said he would be waiting for you when you cross over. Then he fluttered his gorgeous wings and flew off to play with all the other angels."

I remembered the beautiful voice of Grandma as I put my books aside. Apparently, unconditional love wasn't a new concept at all, except for us mere humans.

13

The Chosen

Come unto me, all ye that labor and are heavy-laden, and I will give you rest.

Matt. 11:28

Barry Larson didn't fit in no matter where he was. He grew up in a violent home—"house" would be more correct, I suppose—and learned early the terrible pain of fear. In the winter, Barry never took his coat off, even when he was inside, because he wanted to be ready to run outside when his father went into his terrifying fits of rage brought on by alcohol. There had been many times that emergency room personnel had seen the bruises on his tiny body, but they had "believed" the lies of his father, rather than spend their off days in a courtroom somewhere testifying about what they had seen. They didn't want to get involved.

Barry went off to grammar school, which was a blessed relief for him. The fights of his mother and father would go on late into the night, as he cowered beneath his covers waiting for the sunlight to come. He needed no one to wake him up; his internal alarm clock did just fine. He dressed himself and was ready to go long before his mother stumbled into his room. Many a morning he walked to school while his parents were still asleep. School was his place of safety, or should have been.

Barry sat in the classroom with a dazed look in his eyes, wearing clothes that were old and didn't match. His hair was in tangles, and it was obvious he hadn't bathed. He never seemed to have the right answers when he was called upon, and after a time he stopped raising his hand. He needed special attention, but he wasn't a favorite of his teachers. They hadn't learned to love the unlovable, so they mainly just tolerated him. So,

each day, Barry was the first one at school and the last
to leave, but it was as though he was not really there at
all. Somebody should have asked about his empty stomach, but they didn't. Somebody should have asked about
his empty heart, but they didn't. When the children went
to play and sides were chosen, Barry was always the last
one taken. The children had learned how to love a winner, but by this standard, Barry wasn't very lovable.
Barry didn't understand what was happening, and he
withdrew into himself more and more as time went by.
Somebody should have seen the crusted blood on his
nose, not just the snot that he was told to wipe off.
Somebody should have seen the bruises on his arms that
lay in surrender by his sides. It wasn't that people were
blind; they just didn't want to get involved.

By the time Barry got to high school, it seemed he
had lived a hundred years. He had seen things children
should never see, or adults for that matter. Yet, he perse-
vered as best he could. He was an easy target for
teenage ridicule, but by now he knew how to smile and
keep on going. He no longer had bruises on the outside
of his body, but the scars on the inside more than made
up for it. He tried out for the baseball team but wasn't
chosen. He tried out for the band but didn't make it
there, either. Once he wrote a poem that the English
teacher praised. It was beautiful for sure, seeing as how
Barry's pain had given him the soul of a poet. But his
fellow students laughed at him and called him "queer,"
and he never wrote another one. By his senior year, he
was shooting heroin through his veins and sitting in
class like a zombie. Maybe somebody should have inter-
vened. But he wasn't causing any trouble, so nobody
wanted to get involved.

When Barry left high school, he took up with another

young man, and they became lovers. He didn't care if people called him names—for once in his life he had found someone who sincerely cared for him. The relationship grew strong, but Barry grew weak. The doctor made the diagnosis of AIDS, and Barry went to the free clinic for treatment. But the virus still took its toll. In his sickness he found God, but the church preferred he just get lost.

Barry was not much more than a shadow with a soul that day he started home from the clinic. A group of gang members saw him, and for one of the few times in his whole life, he was chosen. They beat him to death with baseball bats, spitting the words "faggot" and "queer" into his face as they stood over him. A crowd of people watched this terrible crime taking place, but not one person tried to stop it. They didn't want to get involved. Barry's life had now come full circle as he lay there dying on that concrete.

Someday, when these brief moments we call life are over, I'm sure we'll be standing in line at the pearly gates, praying that we get chosen by the One who's always involved. Somehow, I can't imagine God not choosing Barry Larson to be on His team.

14

There's No Place
Like Home

When a finger points at the moon, the imbecile looks at the finger.

Chinese proverb

Whenever a man does a thoroughly stupid thing, it is always from the noblest motive.

Oscar Wilde

If "stupid is as stupid does," then I was really stupid. In 1961, I was playing minor league baseball in the Sophomore League in El Paso, Texas, a league composed of cities in Texas and New Mexico. I didn't know it then, but the word *sophomore* literally means "wise moron." That was the way I was that night for sure, and I had about 5,000 witnesses.

It was bat night, and the opposing El Paso team was giving away bats to all youngsters attending the game. It was a good promotion, and people trickled through the turnstiles until there was a flood of folks filling up the seats in the old ballpark. I had pitched the night before, and the crowd then was about 300 die-hard fans, the usual minor league attendance. But this crowd was huge. I was sitting in the bullpen in case I was needed as a relief pitcher for a few innings. I had my black satin-sheen Pittsburgh jacket on and was daydreaming about someday being in the major leagues. I like to blame the incident on my daydreaming, but total lack of concentration is more accurate.

Somewhere around the eighth inning of a very boring game, the substitute second baseman ran from the third-base dugout to the bullpen along the left-field foul line and hollered, "Hey, Eades, Skipper wants you to coach first base. Get us some runs." Still in the daze of my daydreaming, I took off for the first-base coaching box, not looking up until I got there.

Once in the coaching box, I buttoned up my jacket, hitched up my pants, and started clapping my hands and saying something like, "All right, let's get some runs!" I felt important as I glanced up at all those fans. Now I was a part of the big event. I didn't chew tobacco, but I remember spitting on the dirt in the coaching box. It seemed the manly thing to do. And besides, I had been chosen to coach first base, and that was an important assignment. It was then, out of the corner of my eye, that I saw an El Paso player coming toward the coaching box.

"What are you doing here?" he asked me.

"I'm coaching first base, you idiot," I responded in an arrogant manner, feeling my oats.

"Well, why don't you look out in the field, stupid," he said, spitting real tobacco juice near my shoes.

I looked out in the field, and there I saw my first baseman, my second baseman—in fact, the whole team. It didn't take a Rhodes scholar to realize the other team was at bat. I had been had. The substitute second baseman had been playing a practical joke. A practical person would have caught it immediately. But me, my thoughts had been somewhere above the bright stadium lights, and I had stood in that coaching box like a baby deer mesmerized by the headlights of a car. Now I was run over by the reality of my situation. The crowd had picked up on my blunder and started jeering, and I just couldn't make myself run back over to the third-base dugout in front of them. So—and to this day I don't know why—I took off running full speed toward second base and slid into the bag, just as my pitcher finished his warm-up tosses and my catcher threw the ball to the second baseman to begin the inning.

The second baseman was stunned. "What in the hell are you doing, Eades?"

I got up and dusted off my pants. "I don't know," I said, and that was the gospel truth. At this point, I heard the crowd cheering. I figured I might as well make the best of it. I tore out for third base like a runaway rhino.

It was the best hook slide I had ever done in my life. Now the crowd was really cheering, but above their noise I could hear the angry voice of my manager, Al Kowalski, as he yelled at me from the top of the steps in the third-base dugout. His face was an awful thing to see.

"Get in this dugout! Now!" he kept repeating, making every parental gesture I had ever seen. I was too scared to go into the dugout. The crowd chanted, "Steal home, steal home, steal home!" They were laughing and cheering, and that seemed a whole lot better than staying at third base, especially since Mr. Kowalski was now coming out onto the field toward me. I took off for home plate.

It was a headfirst slide, probably a submissive suicide gesture on my part. By now, the home-plate umpire had joined in the festivities, and he screamed, "Safe!" as my hand went across the plate. I stood up, dusted myself off and tipped my hat to the fans, who were giving me a standing ovation.

It is true that you can only run so far. I knew I had to go to the dugout, and I did, much like a condemned man trudging toward his date with destiny and doom. I looked up to see Mr. Kowalski laughing. "This was bat night, Eades, not batty night," he said with a broad grin. I laughed, too, mostly out of relief. He was the governor, and he had just commuted my sentence, at least for that night.

15
No Titles

To pity distress is but human; to relieve it is Godlike.

Horace Mann

am was a gentle giant of a man who roamed the wooded backlands of Kentucky. He was an oak that God Himself had carved His initials into as a sapling, and those sacred scars could be seen by anyone who spent even a few moments around him. Tall and strong, he stood with a wisdom that must have made the mountain owls wonder if perhaps they had been slighted in some way during that very first week of creation.

He had gone off to work in the coal mines when he was still too young to shave and toiled there in the tunnels until blessed retirement came. It had been a hard life, full of pressure. Coal mining's always like that, and leaves many a man as black and broken as the coal he hauls up. But not Sam. When he came up out of the mines having to return no more, it seems the pressure and time had merely combined to transform him into a human diamond that sparkled in the sacred sunshine above the ground. He had given the coal owners their money's worth and now was free to spend his days giving the coal maker's His.

A man once said that in the Bible, Paul had the titles but Timothy had the testimony. Timothy was a kind-hearted man who saw the best in the disciples, even when Paul was chewing them out for falling short of what was expected of them. He was a peacemaker and friend in hard times. One can only imagine that when Timothy left this earth, people gathered about at his funeral giving testimony about what he had done for them. Way into the night, the friends of Timothy must have stood in circles, waiting for one man to end his account of the generosity of Timothy's spirit so another could begin. Nobody would have read off a list of Timothy's titles—he had none—but they would have celebrated the life of this man who was a living testimony to the teachings of Christ. So it was when Sam died.

The funeral was over, but not a soul had left the cemetery. Sam was such a good man that many of them figured they might actually see him rising up into the heavens. Finally, the women said they would go prepare some food, seeing as how the fingers of night were wrapping around the old graveyard. The men said they'd be along directly, but taking off their topcoats, they instead sat on the ground three deep in a circle. It seemed every man in the county had come to pay his respects.

H. C. Horton was the first to speak. "I know ya'll don't know this 'cause old Sam wouldn't ever say nary a word about it. But one time I was laid off at the mine and didn't have two pennies to rub together, and he just shows up one day in that old pickup of his right outside my house. He had a big canvas spread over the bed of his truck and asked me if I'd do him a favor. I told him sure, what was it? Sam said he'd been a fool and planted too much food. He was afraid it was going to spoil, and he'd feel like a bigger fool for being wasteful. He said to me, 'H. C., you'd really be doing me a fine favor if you'd agree to take this stuff off my hands.'"

H. C. choked up when he said to the huge circle of men, "We were so hungry and so broke, and when I said I'd do it, he shook my hand like I'd saved him from this awful disgrace. Sam pulled that canvas off and asked me if I'd mind helping him carry the food inside. Can you believe that—he asked *me* if I'd mind. When I saw what was in the bed of that truck, I couldn't believe it. Hundreds of ears of corn and tomatoes—must have been 200 of those—and baskets and baskets of beans and okra and peas. We carried that food into the house with Sam thanking me every step of the way. The last thing he brought in was a huge burlap sack. I asked him what it was and he said I'd need something to season the beans with. I must have been in shock 'cause I plumb forgot to shake his hand. The only thing I shook was my head when I opened that sack and saw what must have been a whole hog in there. I'm telling you, if Christ left any footprints on this earth, then Sam sure walked in them." Amens rose into the darkening sky. Bill Pitts brought a kerosene lamp from his truck, lit it and placed it in the midst of the men.

Mr. Williams asked one of the men to help him to his feet and stand by him to hold him up. Mr. Williams was 101, with a long white beard that was about as wide as his frail body. He spoke to the respectfully silent men.

"Ya'll know I loved to go to church. Then I had this stroke and couldn't walk anymore. Well, I'm laying in bed feeling sorry for myself one Sunday morning, about ready to give up the ghost, when in walks Sam, who quickly tells me it's his 80th birthday before I can start complaining too much. He then tells me he figures it's time he starts going to church, seeing as how he was getting old and all, and said it might as well be the one I went to, so he was there to carry me to church. I tried to complain, but ya'll know Sam. He agreed with every word I was saying, and all the time he was busy putting my Sunday best on me. When I was dressed, he went into the bathroom, came back with a wet comb, and slicked my hair and beard like I was some kind of doll in the country store. Then, the next thing I know, he's picked me up in his arms and is carrying me outside. He places me in the front seat of his truck like I'm some special-delivery package from the post office, and off we go. I never will forget the way people turned and looked at us that day when he carried me into the church. He did that every Sunday until the day he died. When Sam said he was going to carry you to church, he really meant it!" The men chuckled low, more in acknowledgment than amusement.

"I'm going to miss him," Mr. Williams said, looking at the now star-filled sky, "and I don't believe there's enough stars to match the good deeds of this man. Well, I reckon I've said enough, but it seems I had something else to say." He rubbed his white head for a moment, then his eyes sparkled like the stars. "Oh, yeah, I remember now. I can't wait for God to hold me close to His bosom so I can feel as loved as I did when Sam carried me in his arms."

Mr. Williams sat down, and one by one the others stood, giving their testimony about Sam. Finally, each man having said his piece, they lingered, then left Sam to the quiet of the night. His spirit had fallen upon them like the dew, soaking them in sweet memories.

Sam had no titles, he left no large sum of money and he wasn't famous. All he left was something that titles, money and fame can't buy—he left a legacy of love.

16

The Road Back

In time of war, the devil makes more room in hell.

German proverb

"**S**piderman" owned a Harley and any piece of ground he was standing on when you met him. He had more tattoos than a fleet of sailors, but it was the cobweb ones on his elbows that gave birth to his nickname. Surely he had a real name, but nobody knew what it was or dared to ask. Sometimes, when trying to soften the image of an imposing adult, you can try to imagine what that person may have looked like as a child. This technique didn't work when you were around Spiderman. No matter how much effort you expended, it was impossible to see him as any way but the way he was. And what he was, was absolutely frightening.

Many Harley riders are like M&Ms on motorcycles. They have a hard shell on the outside but are soft and sweet on the inside. However, Spiderman was a man who seemed to be composed of thousands of shells layered one on top of the other, and nobody knew what lay at his very core. It was doubtful that he himself knew the answer to that.

He was huge and solid, with a dark black beard and long hair, which he wore in a braided ponytail. His thick black eyebrows fused together above his sharp nose and sheltered the demonic eyes beneath them. It was as though he had gone to hell, ripped out the devil's eyes and placed them in the sockets below his black caterpillar eyebrows. Maybe, in a way, Spiderman had made this trip to Satan's soil. Frank said he had, and Frank knew him best of all.

Frank and I used to ride our Harleys together, and

now and then we'd be joined by Spiderman, who would just happen by. He would come roaring up beside us and acknowledge us by lifting one finger up from his grip on his handlebars. It wasn't much of a greeting, but at least it was his way of letting us know he knew we existed.

One day we three rode together on back roads for almost an hour. Frank and I pulled off at an old country store to get a cold drink, but Spiderman just kept on going, without even a wave good-bye. Frank and I removed our helmets.

"That Spiderman sure is a strange guy," I said to Frank, as I placed my helmet on the rearview mirror.

"Only way he could be," Frank answered, as we went inside to get our drinks. We came back out and sat on the wooden bench on the side of the store.

I continued the conversation. "What did you mean, Frank, about Spiderman being the only way he could be?"

"Well," Frank said, as he set his drink on the bench and lit a cigarette, "you have to understand that Spiderman is a Vietnam veteran who spent three years as a prisoner of war and saw things that human eyes aren't supposed to see. He was subjected to inhuman punishment and regularly sees a psychiatrist over at the VA."

"Does he have post-traumatic stress syndrome?" I asked, and Frank looked at me in a strange way, seeing as how I had stated the obvious. But he was tolerant of my book learning.

"Well, that's what the shrinks say, but that's just a human trait, always putting a label on something as though that makes it understandable. What I think is that he's got the same thing I had when I came back from Vietnam."

"What's that, Frank?" I asked, as his eyes stared into the fields across the road.

Then Frank spoke. "It's hard to describe, to put into words that make sense, if you know what I mean. I guess it's like there was this beautiful part of me that something stole from me when I was over there and replaced it with something ugly that I brought home. Do you understand?"

"Sort of," I answered, but he probably saw the confusion in my eyes.

"Look," Frank said, "it's like this. I had this angel of hope I lost over there, and I found, although I wasn't searching for it, a demon of despair that burrowed into my very soul. I think Spiderman's just got a worse case than I had." Frank finished with a strong sigh.

"How did you get over it, Frank?" I questioned.

"I'm not sure I did," he answered with a thin smile, "but it got better with a whole lot of praying and friends who were there for me when I needed them." As he put on his helmet, he added, "It's hard to think with all the noise from my Harley. So, I ride a lot. Makes me feel free for a while, too."

We were on our way back when Spiderman caught up with us once again, seeming to come out of nowhere. I noticed his Harley was the loudest of all, and maybe that's exactly the way it was supposed to be.

17
The Miracle He Missed

Miracles are missed more often than
trains. People look for trains.

Anonymous

He didn't want salvation because his sins were all he had, especially for recreation, and he didn't care to have anyone take them away. It was rain that drove him inside the church that day, not some spiritual search or longing for meaning and sense in his life. The huge raindrops were making Dalmatian spots on the pristine white concrete steps of St. Dominic's as he darted up them. The building could have been a garage for all he cared; he was seeking shelter, nothing else. He entered through solid oak doors made for giants, doors that he was sure no human could ever be tall enough to fill.

Lionel Suddeth flicked the raindrops from his suit and briefcase as he sat down on a pew next to a light on the right wall and opened the newspaper to the obituary section. The long list of names of the recently deceased pleased him. He ran one of the oldest scams around.

Lionel was a Bible salesman of sorts, and Bibles could be seen bulging out of his briefcase with the broken zipper. His was an old, simple con that preyed upon widows. He'd look up a deceased man's name in the obituary section and make a call on the grieving wife. Lionel would arrive at her front door with the big red Bible prominently held against his heart, like he might be a preacher, and would ask for the dead man. He'd feign shock when he was informed that the man had died. Then, with practiced precision and timing, he would say, "I'm so sorry to hear that. He was such a good man. He had ordered this collector's edition Bible from me, and it took longer to get them in than we expected. If only

113

they had come in sooner. He said it was a special gift for
his wife."

At this point, Lionel would actually say the woman's
name, which he had found in the paper. It had a ring of
authenticity and usually got the wife's attention as he
apologetically said, "I'm sorry to have come here in your
grief. I'll just cancel the sale. God knows I wouldn't
want to collect for a Bible that you never got the chance
to receive from your husband."

Lionel would then turn to leave the porch. But more
likely than not, he wouldn't make it down the steps
before the wife called him back and, with tears in her
eyes, purchased the expensive Bible.

Lionel Suddeth was a professional confidence man
who used the Bible and God's name as unholy trumps
in his seedy game of making money from tragedy.

The church doors opened once more, as a gray-haired
old woman with a shawl over her head slowly shuffled
in and sat on the pew directly in front of him. Her
clothes were damp, and the wetness activated the smell
of mothballs. She knelt and prayed as Lionel pored over
the names in the newspaper, preparing a list of his next
victims, putting checks beside their names. It was an
odd scene. The sacred and the slick were within arm's
reach of each other.

The woman finished her prayer, crossed herself, and
rising to leave, turned and looked over her shoulder at
him.

"I remember you," she said softly. "You're that sweet
Bible salesman that I bought the Bible from. You
remember, the one my precious Burl ordered right
before he died. The big red one, the collector's edition.
Do you remember me?"

"Oh, yes," Lionel answered, although he couldn't ever

remember having seen her. "Sure, I remember you. I guess it was the shawl that threw me off for a moment. How have you been doing?"

"Good as could be expected, I suppose. I'm so happy to have run into you. Please give me your name again," she said.

"Lionel. Lionel Suddeth," he said, smiling. "And yours?"

"Edith Swanson," she answered.

"This sure is a beautiful church, Mrs. Swanson. Are you a member here?" he inquired.

"I sure am," she said. "I come here every day and pray. It brings me great comfort and peace. It's a regular habit of mine. You know, just yesterday I prayed that I might see you again to thank you for all you did for me. That red Bible may have cost me almost $200, but it has been a marvelous blessing!"

Mrs. Swanson reached into her oversize handbag and pulled it out. "I know you might think I'm a silly old woman, but I carry it with me everywhere I go. To tell you the truth, I even sleep with it nestled right there on Burl's pillow. I hope I get to keep it." She spoke with a profound sadness in her eyes.

"You hope you get to keep it?" Lionel had a quizzical expression on his face. "What do you mean?"

"Well, I have to take it by the diocese this afternoon. The bishop himself has requested to see it," she answered.

"What does he want to see it for?" Lionel asked, feeling more paranoid than curious. "I mean, nothing's wrong, is it?"

"Oh my, no, Mr. Suddeth," she assured him. "Just the opposite. Well, I've taken enough of your time. I better be on my way. It's been wonderful seeing you once again." She walked down the length of the pew and up the padded aisle toward the huge doors.

Lionel folded the newspaper into his briefcase and hurried after her, catching up with her before she started down the steps. It had stopped raining, and the sunshine glistened off her silver hair and aged but angelic face.

Catching his breath, Lionel said, "Say, Mrs. Swanson, I was just wondering why the bishop wanted to see your Bible. We got to talking, and you never did say."

She paused for a moment, then walked up close to him and in a low voice asked, "Did you ever hear of the Shroud of Turin?"

Lionel read the papers; he was well informed of the news. "Sure," he said. "Wasn't that the burial cloth of Christ that had His image embedded in it? I read where they were trying to determine if it was authentic."

"Exactly," Mrs. Swanson said. "Well, that's precisely why the bishop wants to see my Bible."

"I'm still confused," Lionel responded. "Please tell me what you're talking about."

"Well, you must promise you'll never tell a soul," Mrs. Swanson said in a whisper.

"I won't!" he promised.

"Alright, then," she said. "Well, about a week after I bought that red Bible from you, I noticed something strange about the inside back cover of it. At first, I thought maybe it was just an old brand that had been on the cow used to make the leather cover. But every day it got larger and more defined. You know, like a negative being developed. As more days passed, it took on a more clear definition, until finally I knew for certain what it was. Look, I'll show you!" Mrs. Swanson pulled the Bible from her handbag and turned to the inside back cover. It was the image of Christ's face.

Lionel was amazed. He examined the Bible closely but had no idea as to how the image had been made. It was

almost three-dimensional and had a hologram quality to
it. He stood there more stunned than skeptical.

"That's unbelievable!" he finally said, as he handed the
Bible back to a beaming Mrs. Swanson.

"It's more than that—it may even be a miracle. That's
why the bishop wants to study it. If it appears to be
authentic, the diocese will give me $1,000 for it. Then
they can examine it for possible exhibit at the church
museum. Of course, if there is a rational explanation for
it, they won't give me any money at all, but I'm sure it's
a divine act. Don't you think so?"

"I don't know much about these kinds of things,"
Lionel answered, "but I guess it's possible."

Mrs. Swanson looked down at the concrete. "It's just
got to be real. My daughter needs a serious operation,
and I really need the money. Mrs. Everson's seen it,
bless her soul. Her husband just died, and she thinks it's
a real miracle. She said she'll give me $2,000 for it if the
church rejects it, but I'd hate to take her money. She's
not well off, you know."

Lionel recognized the name Everson. He'd put a check
by it in the paper not more than five minutes ago. His
mind worked fast as he spoke. "I hate to say this, Mrs.
Swanson, but if the church rejects it, I don't think you're
the kind of lady who would take $2,000 from a
struggling widow woman like Mrs. Everson."

"I guess you're right, Mr. Suddeth. Maybe I'll just keep
it and try to raise the money for my daughter some
other way. You can't put a price on a miracle, you
know. I feel ashamed for trying to take advantage of
God's handiwork." She shrugged her shoulders and
started down the steps, but he called her back, crocodile
tears in his eyes.

"Look, Mrs. Swanson, I'll tell you what. There's no

need to take a chance on the church rejecting your
Bible. I know you need the money, and I'm willing to
take the risk, even if it's not authentic, and offer you
$500 cash for it. Anytime you want to see it, you can just
come by." He handed her a business card with a phony
address on it.

Mrs. Swanson cried as she spoke. "Maybe the miracle
was my running into you today. Perhaps this is exactly
what God intended."

"I'm sure it is," Lionel sweetly said, as he calculated
how long it would take him to get to Mrs. Everson's
house.

"I can come and see it anytime I want?" she asked.

"My door will always be open," he promised.

"Okay, then," she sighed, "I'll do it."

Lionel counted out five $100 bills, and she took one
last long look at the image on the red Bible, then gently
handed it to him. "Please take good care of it," she
pleaded.

"I will," he said, as she turned and eased herself down
the steps and shuffled off up the street, around the corner and out of sight.

Whatever plans Lionel had had for the red Bible evap-
orated as quickly as the raindrops on the hot pavement.
As his fingers once again traced the image of Christ, they
began to tingle, and a burning sensation rose up his
arms. He began sweating, and his body trembled and
grew weak. At first, he thought he was having a heart
attack, but it was worse than that. Against his will, he
began recalling the awful way he had lived his life.

As he stared down at the image of Christ, the faces of
the widows he had swindled appeared in its place. He
was overcome with a strange feeling that he remembered from long ago. It was guilt. Lionel Suddeth was

overcome by guilt. Suddenly, a gust of wind furiously blew the pages of the red Bible until they came to rest on John 3:16, and he read, "For God so loved the world . . . "

There was no doubt in his mind. He was convinced he was holding a true miracle in his hands. He walked back into the church and knelt at the altar, where he received Christ that very day. Lionel left his briefcase containing the Bibles and his newspaper right there beside the altar, and left St. Dominic's with the miracle Bible in his hands and the miracle of salvation in his heart. He felt so tall that he ducked as he went through the huge oak doors.

It was a miraculous day alright. But perhaps the greatest miracle of that day was that God had blinded Lionel Suddeth so he couldn't see that Mrs. Swanson was a Bible salesman just like he had been.

18

A Valentine
Above the Valley

Living high up in the mountains is a
darn good thing. When you need God,
he ain't got far to go.

Moses July Boggs

he February rain beat its deafening drops upon the tin-roofed building. The structure was more suitable for storage than surgery, but it was where Benjamin Myers performed his medical miracles, so neither he nor his patients paid it much mind. Dr. Ben, as the local mountain people called him, had learned long ago it was more important what went on inside than outside, whether it was buildings or people. So he continued to cut, shape and sew as thunder shook the place, until it rattled like an old tambourine in the hands of a young zealot.

In the shadows of the mountains, Dr. Ben had found the light. In the thickest of forests, he had found a clearing for his mind. This was his seventh year in the Appalachians, and Hobbs Hill was home, especially for his heart. He tied off the last stitch, stood back from the table and stared down at the unconscious boy. Dr. Ben removed his mask and smiled, for he knew the cleft palate operation had been a success. Life would forever be different for his young patient, who would now look and sound normal. Ben said a sincere thank you to God, then asked nurse Lydia to take over. Benjamin Myers walked out onto the small stoop in front of the building and smelled the freshness of the earth. In his mind, he knew he was in the right place, but that hadn't always been the case.

When Ben was nine years old, he and Stray, his new puppy, were asleep. Startled awake by fire and smoke, he grabbed Stray and ran toward the bedroom door, but the intense heat forced him back. It was then that Ben made a decision that would affect him forever. With panic and heroism that only an innocent boy could possibly possess, he held Stray close to his chest as the flames spread quickly throughout the small bedroom. Then, with no hesitation, he ran toward the closed window in the room and dove through the flaming curtain. The curtain wrapped around him like a flaming snake as he burst through the window, shattering the glass. He fell between two firemen who had been poised to break the window with axes to attempt the rescue. Quickly they smothered the flames with their blankets as Stray, frightened but unharmed, ran off into the yard. But the polyester curtain fabric burned fast and hot. Ten more seconds, and Ben would have been rescued. But instead, his face was burned and cut beyond recognition. He was disfigured for life, left with permanent scars both inside and outside. Fate had changed his life forever.

Five reconstructive surgeries brought pain and depression, but minimal improvement to Ben's disfigurement. The surgeons were very competent, but the tissue damage was too severe and extensive. Ben's face now resembled some grotesque jigsaw puzzle, but his mother's love was steadfast and deep. The depth of her love was never more evident than the day when Ben finally came home from the hospital following his fifth surgery. It was morning, and Mr. Myers had left for work. Mrs. Myers was in the kitchen alone when Ben quietly padded into the room, tugged on her apron, looked up at her face like some small, lost puppy and said, "Momma?"

"What is it, sweetie?" she asked.

"Momma, I've been thinking. If it's okay with you and Daddy, I'd just as soon not have any more surgery. Is that okay?"

Mrs. Myers knelt down and, lovingly holding him by the shoulders, said, "Okay, Ben, no more surgeries."

Benjamin Myers grew up in a different way from most children. He avoided mirrors and took to wearing a cap pulled down low over his forehead to hide his face. He never again received a Valentine's Day card at school, never played sports, never had a girlfriend and never felt at ease anywhere but in his room reading, where he developed his brain until he was brilliant. He may have been scarred beyond recognition, but anyone could recognize that brilliance.

One night after supper, 13-year-old Ben and his father sat around the table talking. "Daddy," Ben said, "you know what I wish?"

"What's that, Son?" his father answered, sipping his hot coffee.

"I wish I were one of those heroes who gets to wear a mask," Ben replied. "You know, Daddy, like Batman or the Lone Ranger or even Zorro. Nobody sees their faces. And they're brave and are always doing good things for people, and people really like them." Ben hesitated for a moment, trying to find the right words. "I'm sorry, Daddy; I mean, I know they're not real people, but I just wanted to tell you what I was thinking. Guess you think I'm being childish, huh?"

Aaron Myers furrowed his brow, finished off his coffee and smiled. "Well, Ben, I think you might just have a great idea," he said. "So, I guess I hear you saying you want to wear a mask, be a hero, and be admired and liked by people for doing good deeds. Well, if that's the case, Ben, I think I know exactly what you need to do!"

Ben's eyes widened. "Tell me, tell me! What is it, Daddy?"

"The way I see it, Son, you need to become a surgeon."

Aaron Myers, with a stroke of genius, had swung life's pendulum once again. In less than 10 seconds, the pendulum once again affected Ben forever. "I can actually see it now," Mr. Myers continued, staring into space. "Benjamin W. Myers, M.D., surgeon."

From that day forward, Ben was obsessed with making his father's words a reality. Years of dedication and study followed, and when Ben was 28, the dream reached its finish line. Benjamin W. Myers was a medical doctor and a board certified reconstructive surgeon. Yet, even though the dream was a reality, it had turned into a nightmare.

The young Dr. Myers was so physically repugnant that his private practice failed. Plastic surgeons weren't supposed to look like monsters. He closed up his office and came home.

"I'm like a toothless dentist," he told his father over supper one night. "It's impossible to be accepted when people think you should be starring in *Phantom of the Opera*." Aaron Myers saw his son's anguish. He measured his words carefully as he prayed for one more recipe of resolution. "Son, they are always begging for doctors in rural areas. Maybe that's the answer. No frills, little money; just country, not country clubs. Maybe someplace in the Appalachians. I think you would be appreciated there. You should try it, Ben. There's nothing to lose."

That conversation occurred seven years ago. Now, the rain had stopped. Levi and Sarah Staples had visited with their son once nurse Lydia gave them the okay, and now they came out onto the porch to join Dr. Ben. "It's a miracle," Mrs. Staples said in a solemn tone. "God sure works miracles through those hands of yours, Dr. Ben," she said, taking his hands in hers. "We'uns ain't never gwine to be able to thank you enough." She almost bowed as she eased his hands back down with tears in her eyes. "My boy, Adam, why he's gwine to be brand new. Bless you, bless you, bless you, Dr. Ben."

Ben put his hand on her shoulder and squeezed, then turned toward Levi to shake his extended hand. Mr. Staples's hand was like the root of a mountain tree, gnarled and strong. "Adam will be ready to come home in about three days, Mr. Staples. He's going to do just fine."

Levi Staples held Ben's hand for a long time, as though he just couldn't let it go until he said some right words. He chewed on his tobacco, struggled, then said, "Dr. Ben, I's always heard that no man has ever done seen the face of God. But if'n he could, I reckon He'd be a-looking a lot like you." Ben felt embarrassed but knew Levi was speaking heart words, so he didn't dare refute them. Dr. Ben simply smiled and said, "Thank you, Mr. Staples."

Levi, like his wife, cautiously eased Dr. Ben's hand back down, then with his right hand reached into his overalls and pulled out a handmade card, which he offered to Ben, who took it. The card had all the signatures and marks of the people on Hobbs Hill, and it simply read, "Happy Valentine's Day to Dr. Ben from all us folks on Hobbs Hill. We love you." As Mr. Staples took his wife's arm to lead her down from the porch to go home, he turned around and said to Ben, "I hope you like the card, Dr. Ben. 'Course, we'uns already know for sure that God has done sent you His'n."

19

A Newspaper
and Popsicles

Ah Fortune, what god is more cruel to
us than thou! How thou delightest ever
to make sport of human life!

Horace

The other day when I was buying a newspaper at the rack outside the post office, I heard the bell of a Popsicle truck and turned to watch some young children dashing toward it with their money tightly balled up in their fists. Cookie came to my mind.

Teresa went by the name of Cookie. She was a cocaine addict living in the public housing project of a small Alabama town. She made no pretense of coming to the drug treatment center, where I worked, for noble purposes. She had come to avoid having her children taken from her by the Department of Human Resources for being an unfit mother. She made it plain to the counseling staff that once she completed treatment and the heat was off, she probably was going to smoke crack once again. Cookie didn't mind putting the "con" on the "system" but figured it was useless to try to do the same with us. At least she was being honest, and that was a start.

To support her addiction, Cookie was a prostitute, selling herself for as little as three dollars when she was forced into treatment. She loved crack cocaine more than her seven boys and, for sure, more than herself. It wasn't really a question of weak character. Rather, it was the logical progression of the strength and power that cocaine exerts over the addict. Cookie was like every other crack addict, going to any lengths to get and use cocaine. She was a broken woman, held together only by her defiance. Soon, the pieces would shatter like china on concrete, as she was forced to face the reality of how unmanageable her life had become. Our task was to put the pieces back together to form a recovering Cookie instead of a drugging Cookie. Treatment time went by.

I'm not sure of the exact day I thought she had a chance, but I believe it was that day in a group therapy session. "I'm tired of just being a piece of meat," Cookie said, referring to her life of prostitution. "I have felt so dirty sometimes that I wanted to cut myself open and reach in and wash my insides out." For the first time, she cried.

"Try to talk through your tears, Cookie," I urged her. "You're being real today; remember that. I'm mighty proud of the way you're struggling to get well."

With this, her tears fell upon her worn cotton blouse, forming big splotches where they landed. She made no attempt to reach for the tissue box. It was as though she were finally washing out her insides and wanted nothing to stop that liberating process.

"I hate cocaine," she said in a guttural tone, "and I'll tell you why if you won't think it's silly."

"Nothing you say will be silly," said one of the group members, touching Cookie's arm.

"Well," Cookie said, "what I hate about cocaine is I never even have a quarter to buy a morning newspaper. Ain't that something? I want to be able to buy a news-paper, but I can't. All my money goes to the drug man." It was a small thing, but in Cookie's mind, it was impor-tant. Not a person thought it was silly. "And . . ." Cookie tried to continue but had to stop as her crying intensified and the tears literally soaked her blouse. "And," she finally said, "I hate cocaine most of all because when the Popsicle wagon comes through the neighborhood, I never have enough money to buy my boys a Popsicle. It's like they know I've spent all the money on cocaine, but they never complain. They're good boys. They deserve better from their momma. Someday I'm going to have enough money to buy a newspaper and Popsicles anytime I want to. And I can if I stay off that crack."

Cookie got her children back. She also got herself back. Often, as a former patient, she would come back and sit in on group therapy and tell her story. Her life story was a powerful antidote for other addicts whose souls had been poisoned by crack.

It seemed as if Cookie had been straight forever the last time she came by my office. Cookie stuck her head in my office door and asked if she could come in. She looked strange. Her face was very swollen. "Hey, Dr. John," she said with bright eyes and a smile, "I just wanted to come by and tell you the news before you heard it from somewhere else."

"What's wrong with your face?" I asked her as she sat down.

"Cortisone does that," she answered. "The doctor says it's normal."

"Why are you on cortisone, Cookie, and what's the news you're talking about? You're not back on drugs, are you?"

"Oh, no, Dr. John," she said, "I ain't on crack. I've been off crack for seven years. I'm on cortisone because last year the doctor tested me and found out I have AIDS. He figured I got it when I was out running the streets doing cocaine."

I sat there, not knowing what to say. At that point, life seemed so unjust. Cookie saw the concern in my face and answered the unspoken question.

"Don't worry, Dr. John," she said gently. "I ain't going back to crack. I'm having too much fun with my boys." She glanced at her watch. "Well, I better be going. I've got a doctor's appointment in a few minutes," she said, as she stood up from the chair.

We hugged good-bye. When she got to the door, she turned around and said, "You know, if I hadn't got off that crack, I'd have been dead long ago. So I got nothing to complain about. One day at a time, huh, Dr. John?"

"Right, Cookie, one day at a time," I said, owing the strength in my voice to her acceptance of her situation. The student really had become the teacher.

20

Pink Slips Aren't
Appropriate
for Halloween

The gravity of a situation can pull even
the loftiest to the ground.

Anonymous

Felix Maxwell suffered from depression. He tried to keep his head above water, but his soul sank as though it were in a sack of stones. Sleepless nights left the shadows of fatigue beneath his eyes, to remind him he had taken a beating from life. Felix was frail and weak from the fearful fog of depression that would not lift. As a result, he missed too many days at work. Finally, Mr. Oswald, the store manager, called him in one day, October 31 to be exact, to tell him his services were no longer needed. Felix was depressed, not brain damaged, and he realized he was simply being fired.

"Mr. Oswald," Felix said, "I'm on medication for depression and seeing a local doctor. It won't be long before I'll be good as new." Mr. Oswald stood there listening with his arms crossed because he had already made his decision. Felix continued trying anyway.

"Look, Mr. Oswald," Felix said in a weak voice, "losing my job will only make me more depressed, and I know in your heart you wouldn't want me to go into a deeper depression."

Mr. Oswald replied, "I appreciate what you have to say, Felix, but we have a business to run. My decision to fire you is simply a business decision, and you shouldn't take it so personally." Felix shook his head because to him, being fired was very personal and frightening.

Mr. Oswald stood up, which is management's way of ending a meeting, and said, "Listen, Felix, if there is anything I can do for you in the future, don't hesitate to call on me." Well, this made no sense at all to Felix, who realized he was soon to *have* no future. In desperation, Felix reached out and grabbed Mr. Oswald's arm in a last-ditch effort to get him to change his mind. Felix began talking faster, the way a person does when he realizes the listener is losing patience with the conversation.

"Please, Mr. Oswald," Felix begged. "If I lose my job, I'll have no insurance for the doctor or medications. I might become so bad off that I become suicidal, especially if I lose my house and belongings because I have no income."

When Felix made his last plea, Mr. Oswald lit a cigarette and for the first time since the meeting began, seemed to be contemplating Felix's words.

Poor Felix, always a strict abider of store policy, gently said, "I'm sorry, Mr. Oswald. I know this is the third floor and the manager's offices are here, but it's against the rules to smoke anywhere in the building. Even a supervisor could be fired for such behavior."

Mr. Oswald walked over and raised the window, then casually flicked out his ashes. Felix, who was as open as the window, reminded him once more of the policy, ending with, "You shouldn't do that, Mr. Oswald."

"Position has its privileges!" Oswald sneered, as he turned and glared at Felix. Well, that's probably true. But Mr. Oswald was in a bad position, especially when he yelled at Felix, "I don't care what happens to you! You're fired! Go clear out your desk!"

The ambulance came and went. Nobody could have survived that fall. Strange how nobody knew exactly how depressed Mr. Oswald had been.

21

Treasure the Thought

Nothing on earth consumes a man more
quickly than the passion of resentment.

Friedrich Nietzsche

He remembered it. Who wouldn't remember being 50 miles off the coast, bobbing up and down in shark-infested waters for three days? Travis Bowers would have died had it not been for the large plank of wood that floated his way on the second day. He had wrapped himself around the wood, and something gave him the strength to hold on. That something was a seething anger and resentment that permeated every pore of his body. He was so engrossed in thoughts of revenge that he didn't hear the Coast Guard helicopter until it was almost directly overhead. The Coast Guard crew later remarked that he was the only man they ever rescued who hadn't smiled. That was nine years ago, and Travis Bowers still hadn't smiled. He had spent his days looking for Larry Brooks, and he wouldn't smile until he found him.

Larry Brooks was a dreamer and a schemer, probably a lot more of the latter. He had talked Travis into parting with most of his money and all of his time to seek sunken treasure off the coast of Florida. Larry Brooks had the map, the equipment and the boat, *The Treasure Hunter*, and he brought Travis on as a partner to help him raise the treasure that had gone down with a Spanish sailing ship in the 1700s. Larry was full of conviction and had convinced Travis they would be millionaires when they located the exact spot the sailing ship had gone down, and he was sure they would find it. It was just a matter of time until they hoisted up gold doubloons, jewels and rare, expensive artifacts. The twin engines of *The Treasure Hunter* spun in the water as the two men left port with fantastic dreams of wealth spinning in their minds.

"Nine years is a mighty long time," said the bartender, as he served up another gin and tonic for Travis Bowers.

"You bet it is," Travis said. "But every day I think of a new way to torture that Judas. You sure you never heard of a guy named Larry Brooks? He'd be a big spender for sure. Loved to drink his gin in bars."

"Nah, I'd remember someone like that," the bartender replied. "So tell me again why you hate this guy so much."

Travis took a sip of his drink. "Like I was saying, we finally found the ship 50 miles off the coast. We spent seven days and nights raising her treasure, and I'm telling you, there were millions in gold coins, jewels, fancy statues and artifacts. We had everything on board. I bet you *The Treasure Hunter* was sitting two feet deeper in the water, we were so loaded. The morning of April 11, 1984, we got ready to leave. The engines were running and everything was loaded, when Larry asked me to be sure and check to see if the anchor was secured. The next thing I knew, he shoved me overboard, and he was gone in a flash. Three days later, the Coast Guard rescued me, and I've been everywhere looking for him. Up the East Coast and back down around, through every town on the Gulf. I'll tell you one thing: I'll find him, or I'll die trying." The bartender poured another drink.

But Travis didn't find him, although it seemed parts of himself died trying. He had wasted so much of his life that the venom he was saving for Larry Brooks had overflowed into his own system, making him sick in a way much worse than death itself. He had questioned so many bartenders, but never seemed to question the value of his poisonous pursuit.

Eleven years had passed, and it was in the spring of 1995 when Travis Bowers entered the Pelican Bar and Grill in a small Florida coastal town just after noon. The place was empty, so he chose to sit in a booth where he ordered gin and tonic. There was a local paper folded over, lying on the seat of the booth, and Travis opened it to the sports page.

It probably was best he hadn't bothered to read the front page. The story there was about a local deep-sea fisherman who had snagged a human skull on his line 35 miles offshore, and the Coast Guard had been called to investigate. Their report indicated the recovery of a sunken boat that contained huge quantities of gold coins, jewels and Spanish artifacts, which had been turned over to the federal government. The Coast Guard authorities had theorized that the boat may have been overloaded and swamped at sea. The recovery crew had raised a boat, *The Treasure Hunter*, which was still intact, except for a bow plank that had broken loose, probably when the cargo had shifted. A broken watch was found around the arm bone of the skeleton. It was a very expensive chronograph that gave the day, month and year. The date, April 11, 1984, was displayed on the watch's face. Authorities had identified the boat and the remains as belonging to a Mr. Lawrence Brooks.

Travis finished his drink and the sports pages, paid the waitress and got up to leave. He intended to go over to ask the bartender some questions but could see the bartender was busy unloading and stacking merchandise. Travis decided not to bother him. It probably didn't matter anyway. Before long, someone would surely tell him yes, they had heard of Larry Brooks.

22

Hire Education

A man willing to work, and unable to find work, is perhaps the saddest sight that fortune's inequality exhibits under this sun.

Thomas Carlyle

Job interviews are pure torture. That it is easier to find a job when you have a job is a myth. It is not easier; it just isn't a matter of life and death if you already have a job. If you are unemployed and your creditors are having group therapy in your front yard every day, then it's time to push the panic button. So you put on your best clothes and head down, with your head down, to the local employment agency. They assure you that you have the potential of a Bill Gates (but that doesn't compute in your brain), and they swear they will get you interviews with several Fortune 500 companies. You're not sure what this means, except maybe there are 500 companies with fortunes who are willing to pay you a living wage. So you sign on the dotted line, which means if they help you get a job, then you must pay them a percentage of your salary for a period of time, not to exceed the combined ages of your children. You're desperate and depressed. So you sign this devil's document, and off you go. You have a quarter tank of gas and 50¢ in faith. But it's a start, and you have a little hope.

You sit by the telephone and wait. They don't call. You call them. "We're in the process of lining up some interviews," they say, "and you look really good on paper. We'll be contacting you soon." Your spouse asks how it's going, and you mutter something about "contact paper" and hunker down over your bowl of gruel. The spouse smiles, knowing the pressure you've been under could cook a turkey in three minutes.

In a few days, the agency person calls, makes small talk and asks how you've been doing. You want to tell them that remodeling Tara has taken up all of your time, but instead, you lie and say, "Fine." They say they have several interviews for you and want to know if you can make the times they have arranged. Your pride surfaces and you say, "Let me check my schedule." Of course, the only thing on your schedule is watching the mailbox rust, so you say, "That's fine, no conflict."

The day of the interview you show up 30 minutes early. The company representative is 30 minutes late seeing you. Finally, the secretary ushers you into his office. He is sitting behind a mahogany desk that looks like the flight deck of the USS *Kitty Hawk*. He walks around to meet you. He is wearing alligator shoes, an Armani suit and a white shirt with cuff links. You haven't seen cuff links since the high school prom, but you don't let on because you're trying to look sophisticated and smart standing there in your wash-and-wear suit from Sears and your brown penny loafers with dimes stuck in them to look impressive. Sure, you know your shoes aren't alligator. But you do have shiny money in them, and that's got to count for something.

Every job interview, or so it seems, opens with the gambit, "Tell me a little about yourself." This one does, too. So you do. Meanwhile, he's busy putting check marks in squares on a piece of paper in a folder. You hope he will yell "Bingo!" after a while and get the game over, but he doesn't. He just keeps putting check marks down. Then comes the time for the giant question. "Why do you want to work for our company?" he asks, putting the folder down and staring at your eyes like you're Judas on Judgment Day.

You ramble on about their being a Fortune 500

company and their steady growth being an indicator of intelligent management and offering great potential for advancement for someone willing to dedicate themselves to hard work (and that, you assure him, is something you are willing to do). Finally, the interview is over, he says he will let you know, and the tone of his voice lets you know right then. You leave, go down to the street and use the two dimes from the penny loafers to buy a newspaper for the help-wanted section.

There are a few minutes left on the parking meter, so you sit behind the wheel and wonder. You wonder what would have happened if you had told him the truth. That you were broke, brokenhearted and desperate for a job. That you needed money to feed your family and pay your creditors. That you were a kind and gentle person who could do the job. What if you had pleaded for the opportunity to prove yourself? you wonder. But that would have broken the rules of the game. You put a check mark by a job in the want ads and decide to put quarters in your loafers the next time so you won't look so desperate for a job.

23

A Quarter
for Your Pride

Pride, like the magnet, constantly
points to one object, self; but, unlike
the magnet, it has no attractive pole,
but at all points repels.

Charles Caleb Cotton

He was a young man from Alabama with a lot of young money. He was arrogant, pushy and domineering, and frequently bragged about the millions he had made in the fast-food business. A private Lear jet, owned by an old man, was flying in to bring him up to West Virginia to look at some property for expansion of the young man's restaurants into that state. The old man had old money and felt no need to impress anyone with his accomplishments. He was dignified and kind, and made no attempts to flaunt his good fortune. They spent several days looking over many of the old man's properties. Then the elderly man, who was a member of that exclusive golf club in Augusta, Georgia, invited the younger one to fly over with him for a day of golf on the way back to Alabama. The invitation was accepted.

On the first tee, the man from Alabama suggested they play for $100 a hole. He was hoping to impress the others in the foursome, and when the aging man from West Virginia said 50¢ a hole was the most he ever bet, a smug smile crossed the wrinkle-free face of the Alabamian. He was a master of one-upmanship and felt he had succeeded in making the aging man look bad.

When they finished playing golf, the foursome went back to the storied clubhouse for lunch. After eating, they decided to play gin rummy for a while. The grandfatherly gentleman from West Virginia was shuffling the cards when the Alabamian suggested they play for a dollar a point. He was informed that a penny a point was sufficient, as the somewhat embarrassed elder man dealt

the cards. The conversation during the game was punc-
tuated by the brash bragging of the younger man, who
seemed intent on dominating the conversation as well as
the men sitting at the table. Finally, it was time to leave
and transport the man home to Alabama.

The Lear jet had taken off, and the two men sat facing
each other. The Alabamian said he was going to buy a
Lear jet for himself, but he was going to get a much
bigger one so he could carry more people. At this, the
older man called for the copilot to come to the back of
the plane for a moment. The copilot did, sitting down
across the aisle from them, wondering why he had been
summoned.

"Do you have a quarter on you?" the old man asked
the man from Alabama.

"Sure I have a quarter!" the young man replied, pulling
one from his pocket.

"How much money do you reckon you're worth?" he
asked the Alabamian.

"At least $35 million!" he replied in a loud voice.

"Good," the old man said, looking him straight in the
eye. "I'll flip you for it, and the copilot can verify the
winner."

The Alabamian swallowed hard, for he knew the old
man was serious and meant business. The young man
shrugged his shoulders and put the quarter back into his
pocket. The flight was quiet and short, and so was the
man from Alabama.

24

The Panes of Change

It is painful to change. However, when the pain of a situation is greater than the pain of change, then a person changes.

Anonymous

onstance Richardson was definitely a lady, but she had never been a woman. She was prim and proper, and although she had raised two children, she had never raised her voice.

Constance always did the right thing, for she believed it was extremely important to be liked by everybody. She avoided being spontaneous, always thinking of others before she acted, to avoid the risk of offending someone. Constance didn't make waves. Pebble people never make waves. They just lie on the beach with all the other pebbles and let people walk over them. Constance was a pebble who had spent her whole life pretending she was a rock.

She was always baking pies and running errands for neighbors. She never said no to any committee asking her to serve, and showed up with a smile and a dessert. Constance was constant for sure and became a pillar of the community, striving to meet other people's needs but never her own. She felt the "empty nest" syndrome when her children grew up and left home, but only for a little while. All she did was enlarge her nest to include the entire neighborhood for nurturing. Maybe she didn't know this expansion would one day wear her down to the last straw.

Constance was a hybrid human, somewhere between Betty Crocker and Joan of Arc. She was a matronly martyr who everyone said would have plenty of stars in her crown when her life was over. The day her husband, Marvin, ran off with his secretary, it indeed seemed her life had ended.

The day her husband closed the door on their life together, Constance closed the curtains on every window in the house. Her married children's lives went on, but hers had stopped. The children said perhaps it had been a blessing in disguise, seeing as how Marvin had been a tyrant, but Constance didn't hear them. They said she should get out and mingle, letting time heal her heart, but Constance didn't hear them. And, as usually happens, after the initial concern and gossip gathering, married friends stopped coming around and calling to see how she was doing. Her social life left with Marvin, or so it seemed, as she now became a reminder of that terrible reality that might befall her former buddies.

So Constance sat in the dark parlor and rocked, careful to stay on the throw rug so her rocker wouldn't mar the hardwood floor. Good old Constance—from childhood coloring books to rocking chairs, she had always stayed inside the lines.

She never had much practice doing anything just for herself. Now, she was lost. Her mind moved back and forth like her rocker, but it didn't get her anywhere. Constance just rocked. Fall came, and the leaves changed, but not Constance. She just rocked and remembered.

The neighbors said it was sometime in late November, as best they could recollect. That was when it happened—the event that shocked the neighborhood.

Seems a bunch of neighborhood boys were playing in her yard that day, when one of them decided to throw a rock through Mrs. Constance's front window. The youngster must have had a great arm because the rock not only went through the window, but also brought the curtains crashing down.

They stood outside laughing, and then the strangest thing happened. A curtain opened, and another window shattered as the same rock came flying back out of the house at the boys. They started to run, but the boldest one picked up the rock and hurled it through another window of the house. In a minute, the rock came flying back out through a different window. Well, before this game of madness was over, every window in the house was broken.

Then it happened. Constance ran from the front door of the house, screaming she wouldn't take it anymore. The boys knew she meant business because she had Marvin's double-barrel shotgun in her shaking hands. With legs frozen by fear, the boys stood there in her front yard, speechless, as she glared down at them from the porch. Constance cocked the gun, and this time the boys ran like roaches fleeing from a sudden bright light. Suddenly, she whirled, and the blast of buckshot tore the front door off the hinges. Then Constance walked through the doorless portal and packed her clothes.

It was dark when the police car pulled away from the house with Constance in the backseat. Numb neighbors milled around in small groups, talking in hushed tones. They had been shocked into quiet disbelief. But Constance had a broad smile on her face as the squad car pulled away.

The police weren't taking her to jail. After all, she had shot her own house. Instead, they took her to the Greyhound bus station, where she bought a ticket to go to Savannah to be with her sister. There, she opened a catering service that became extremely profitable. She figured she had been catering to everyone her whole life, and it was time people paid her handsomely for it. The winter years of her life were spent in the springtime company of suitors and doing only what suited her.

Constance's children had wanted to repair the house

and sell it, but she wouldn't hear of it. It was to always remain as it was, to symbolize the emotional emptiness of her previous life.

As time went by, young people passed by it at night, but none were brave enough to go up on the old wooden front porch. Many people thought the house was haunted. Some said they could hear the creaking sound of Constance's rocker coming through the doorway and broken windowpanes of the house.

Strange, but when I look back at it, I never was haunted by the house. It was always the memory of sweet old Constance that haunted me. You see, I lived right across the street from her when I was a young boy, not more than a stone's throw away.

25

The Night Before
the Fourth

The things we remember best are those
better forgotten.

Baltasar Gracián

he phone rang. It was late. News that comes late at night is never good, it seems. Still, like Pavlov's dog, I rolled over and responded by lifting the receiver. It was Ken, an old friend, hundreds of miles away from me and thousands of miles away from himself. He had been drinking, was depressed and had dialed me. Getting up with the portable phone, I went to the kitchen table after grabbing a cola from the refrigerator. He needed to talk. Grateful he had called me, I listened.

It was Independence Day eve. Ken was sitting alone on his patio drinking Jack Daniels and swimming in thoughts that even the whiskey couldn't drown. He told me that he was going to the VA for help. He realized he needed to go. He didn't know if that made him a success or a failure as a man. His pain passed over me as I realized he was pulling barbed wire thoughts of the past through his brain.

Ken is kind and gentle, quick to help others and slow to anger. He's a hard worker with an easy smile. It's an awful paradox that such assets can be terrible liabilities, especially when other people take advantage of these good traits precisely because they know they can. Ken's soul was too sweet and slow for the participants in the rat race, who gnawed on him until only a small scrap of his spirit remained.

He was awarded the Purple Heart during the Vietnam War, but he also had those other kinds of scars that can't be seen and take so long to heal, if they ever do. He had been a green kid sucked into the black hole of a war that finally freed his body but took some of his sanity. His first mental breakdown occurred five years after his discharge.

They found him hiding in the cornfield behind his granddaddy's house in the country. He was dressed in his uniform and screaming for the "choppers" to hurry up and land to get the wounded out. His granddaddy, out of breath from running, pushed the stalks of corn aside and knelt down beside him, holding him and crying until the ambulance came. That was 20 years ago. I held the phone tightly as Ken loosened his grip on his memories.

"I broke my promise to God," Ken kept repeating in a plaintive voice. "I was 17 and promised Him when I was wounded and in the mud that if He'd let me live, I'd never do any more bad things the rest of my life. But I didn't keep my promise. I tried, but I just failed." He paused, then hesitantly said, "I also remember crying out for my momma. I was scared and in such pain that all I could think of was God and Momma. What do you think of that?"

"I think I love you, Ken," I said, "and it's because you're a good man. And that's more rare than war heroes."

Ken fell silent; I heard the crickets outside the window. I wished their signals of serenity could fall upon his troubled mind. He didn't speak for what seemed a long time, although it was probably only a few moments. Then, not responding to my words, he continued.

"I've got to tell you something I've never told anyone about. It's about this guy in basic training that I knew." He sighed as he gathered his composure. "His name was Ben Brown, and he was a simple farm boy who couldn't do anything right. He couldn't march, he couldn't shoot and he always failed inspection. He just wasn't cut out to be a soldier and should have been home planting crops or something. If it hadn't been for a war going on, they would have discharged him in two weeks. He didn't have much going for him. Didn't even have a middle initial. One day, the drill sergeant asked him what his middle initial was, and Ben told him he didn't have one. The sergeant kept insisting that everybody had a middle initial, but Ben kept saying he didn't. 'Well, your first name must be Benjamin then,' the sergeant said to him. 'No sir,' Ben answered. 'My first name is Ben and my last name is Brown, and that's all I know. My name is just Ben Brown.'"

I wasn't sure where Ken was going, but I kept my mouth shut so I could follow as he continued. "I tried to help him the best I could, but it didn't do any good. It broke my heart to watch him try so hard. Everybody kidded him, and he'd just smile. He was a good-natured boy and wouldn't harm a fly. One night, I prayed they'd just send him home, but instead they sent him to Vietnam. It was like sending a lamb to slaughter. We all knew he wouldn't stand a chance. So the last day before he's shipped out, he pulls this horseshoe from his foot-locker, and gives it to me, and tells me to take it for good luck, seeing as how I'd been his friend and all. I thanked him. He left for two weeks' leave before being shipped over, and I never saw him again."

"He must have been a nice kid," I said.

"He was that," Ken answered. "Last year, I rode over to Pensacola to the Wall South and was reading the names of those who were killed in Vietnam. I went to the *B*s and read down. Then I saw his name. I ran my fingers across the letters of his name engraved in the granite, and I just started to cry. I couldn't stop crying for Ben

Brown." When Ken said this, he was crying. I gave his sorrow the sacred silence it deserved.

In a few minutes, Ken spoke once again. "I think I've had too much to drink, but I was just thinking how strange it is that we exhale air when we laugh and suck it in when we cry. Listen, I'll call you after I go to the VA."

"I love you, Ken," I said. "Take care of yourself."

"I will," he promised. "I know I need help. Good-bye."

I laid the phone on the table and listened again to the crickets. Ken was right about laughing and crying. I pray that in his crying, he might suck back in some of his soul taken by the black hole of Vietnam. Ken has a Purple Heart. But even more to his credit, he has a good heart.

26

An Angel in Flight

There are defeats more triumphant than victories.

Montaigne

Marcus Rigsby had Down's syndrome, but his momma liked to call it "Ups syndrome" because he always made her feel so happy. He was constantly smiling and dancing, and she said there wasn't an angel anywhere that wouldn't want to have his sweet, innocent face. She was over 40 when he was born and confesses that he wasn't a planned child. But, then again, I suppose that's the case with most of us. Bertrand Russell once said more people are born by accident than die by accident, and he probably made a good point. However, the point of this story is Marcus's first time in the Special Olympics. It was held in the football stadium of the local college several years back, and believe me, it was no accident.

Marcus could run like the wind. His momma said he ran the fastest when she called him to eat, and with a giant grin, he would agree. The truth was, he was a natural who had spent his youth running toward, instead of away from, people. Love makes a person do that, and Marcus was full to the brim with that elusive quality.

Marcus's specialty was running the short sprints, and his anticipation was finally quieted as the big Saturday rolled around. The stadium was full of parents who came to root for their children. They were bonded together in their commonality. The ghosts of boozing and bragging that usually inhabited the stadium had fled in the face of their fellowship. It was a gala day, complete with cheerleaders and a band. There were coaches, timers, officials and volunteers, and it had the air of a professional track meet. There were no clouds except the ones the Special Olympians were walking on. It wasn't the Atlanta Olympics; it was better.

This event was about participating, not about winning or losing. An adult was assigned to each child in the races, and whether that boy or girl finished first or last didn't matter. An adult volunteer waited at the finish line to hug and congratulate each and every one. I'm not sure if championships had anything at all to do with this event, for it seemed, above all else, a convention of the chosen.

The time for Marcus's race arrived. The boys milled around the starting line in their track outfits, waiting for the starter to get them set. There was no psyching each other out with grim faces and attitudes. They were laughing and admiring each other's track attire, pointing and touching, especially those uniforms that were as colorful and bright as the day. Marcus's momma had hand-painted his T-shirt to read "Angel in Flight" across the back. He had insisted on wearing his favorite cut-off jeans because they were "lucky." It took a while, but the starter got them all lined up. Marcus looked down toward the tape at the finish line. Finally, the angelic athletes froze at the starting line as though they were at a dangerous intersection. Then, the starter pointed his pistol in the air and fired. Off they tore down the track— at least most of them did.

Two boys at the starting line just stood there until the kindly adult assistants urged them on down the track. One boy, a very fast one at that, began running toward his parents in the stadium seats before he was ushered back onto the track by volunteers with outstretched arms like the guy in *Catcher in the Rye.*

Meanwhile, Marcus ran straight toward the finish-line

tape. He was faster in fact than Forrest Gump was in fiction. He was no more than 10 yards from winning the race when he looked back over his shoulder to see that his nearest competitor had fallen. Marcus stopped just inches from breaking the tape and, turning around, ran back to help the fallen child to his feet as the other runners sped past him toward the tape. Then, holding each other around the shoulders, Marcus and the other boy ran together toward the waiting adults at the finish line.

They were the last two to finish the race. At first, there was silence, then recognition of what had occurred, then the huge crowd rose to its feet as one and applauded. Not some simple, polite applause that dies quickly, like the kind following a boring speech, but rather, the kind that explodes and rises to a crescendo that does not cease. This convention of the chosen cheered and yelled, and would not stop the thunder of thanks that their hands were making for their heroes with the heavenly hearts.

It's not often that God shows up at a track meet, but He did this day. Every soul there knew it, and they would not sit down or be silenced in their celestial celebration. They clapped until their hands were numb, and they hollered until their voices were hoarse. Then they stomped their feet until enough thunder rose and rumbled through the old stadium that its foundation shook.

Marcus's momma cheered and cried, and then cheered some more. She had raised a child who, in one brief moment of time, had raised the onlookers to heights where they could see beyond mere medallions, maybe even glimpsing the edge of eternity.

I lost touch, and I'm not sure what became of Marcus and his momma, but I hope all has gone well with them. He won't be dancing in some end zone this fall or earning millions of dollars as a professional athlete. He wasn't standing on the winner's pedestal at this past summer Olympics, and maybe it's understandable. You see, they probably could never build a pedestal high enough to honor him. Besides, why would Marcus need a pedestal anyhow? He truly is an *angel in flight*.

27

Better Off As It Was

We would often be sorry if our wishes
were gratified.

Aesop

It was simply a flat tire. It was simply a country road where the simply beautiful girl was standing by her car with a forlorn look that would beckon even the most apathetic person to stop and lend a hand. Yet, it was a truly nice man who rolled to a stop to help her change the tire, not realizing this wouldn't be simply another day in his life.

Fred Holcomb was a kind, gentle man. He hated conflict. But as is often the case, his gentleness betrayed him, and people could see it in his face. He was as vulnerable as a lamb in a wolves' den. So it seemed that just about everyone picked on poor Fred. Oh, he would laugh and go along, but deep inside where the real Fred lived, he was often hurt and afraid. Whatever expressive anger may have remained in his tender soul was never shown. He had learned his childhood lessons very well. He was obedient and docile, and knew anger would bring terrible retaliation from those perceived as more powerful than he. And, to Fred, just about everyone seemed to have more power, courage and intelligence. Yet, no person had tortured Fred as much as he himself. He was a living example of Shakespeare's adage that "Cowards die many times before their deaths; The valiant never taste of death but once." This timid and sweet man, Fred Holcomb, opened his car door and got out to help.

Maria Angelini met him halfway. "I've had a flat. Would you please help me? I'm supposed to have dinner this evening with my father, and he'll just kill me if I'm late." Her smile was beautiful.

"Sure, I'll help you," Fred said. "Just open the trunk and I'll get the spare, the jack and the tire tool. It won't take five minutes," he said, as she popped the trunk lid open. "A beautiful girl like you should never be late for dinner with her father."

Fred was true to his word—it took less than five minutes. He'd had a lot of experience changing flat tires. In truth, it was only when his thin tires with too much mileage blew out that he would buy new tires, and then only one at a time. He wasn't miserly, just miserably short on cash.

Fred put the flat tire, tire tool and jack back into the trunk of Maria's sports car, then closed the trunk lid. She was standing by the open driver's door, ready to go.

"Thank you so very much," she said, extending her hand. Fred wiped his hands on his trousers, then shook hands as he said, "You're more than welcome."

"By the way, do you have a business card?" Maria inquired. "I'm sure my father will want to call and properly thank you."

"Sure I do!" he replied, smiling. He handed her his Matthew's Business Forms business card, which indicated he was a salesman. One more sweet smile and she was gone.

Fred was dreaming a good man's dream that night when the telephone rang. Groggily, he answered. "Are you Fred Holcomb?" the man said, with a voice that could scour a rusty stove.

"Yes sir," he answered, the voice causing him to respond in deference.

"I'm Antonio Angelini," came the deep voice through the earpiece. "You helped my daughter with a flat today?" Fred hesitated before he answered. It then dawned on him that he knew that name. *My God*, he thought, *that's the famous Mob boss!*

Fred "died many deaths" as he recalled telling Angelini's daughter she was beautiful. He could already see the black limousine pulling up outside and two guys named Weasel and Animal breaking his kneecaps with ball-peen hammers. Finally, Fred murmured a weak "Yes, sir."

"Well, you made an old man very happy," he croaked. "I owe you favors."

"Oh, no sir," Fred said gently. "It was really a pleasure for me to be able to help."

"You are too nice a guy," came the vocal gravel once again. "You'll like the favors. Just enjoy!"

It was an order. "Yes sir, Mr. Angelini, I will," Fred said, before laying the phone back on the cradle like he was putting a baby to bed.

By Friday, Fred's world was changing. Banks, restaurants and businesses of all sorts were calling to place orders with Fred's company and demanding, of course, that Fred Holcomb get credit for the sale. Over 100 new accounts had gone to Fred by the end of two weeks. His next commission check was more than he had made all of the previous year. His boss was confused, but of course, very happy. His peers were dumbfounded and extremely jealous, but most of the rude ribbing was no longer aimed at Fred, and, except for Tom Johnson, another salesman, no one continued to pick on Fred.

Fred's anorexic ego fed on the attention he was receiving. He was now beginning to fill out the suit of self-esteem. After a couple of months, his ego was getting too big for his britches. But following years of starvation, Fred was unable to stop gorging himself on the positive attention. Now it seemed he was bulging out everywhere, like a formerly trim athlete who refuses to get larger clothes due to false pride.

It was strange to see that Fred, when he had finally

emerged from his self-made cocoon, had turned out to be a caterpillar instead of a beautiful butterfly. Frankly, he had become obnoxious.

One night, while Fred was lying in bed, wearing his silk pajamas, the telephone rang. He picked it up. "Yeah, what do you want?" Fred said, as he answered the telephone in an arrogant manner.

There was a long silence on the other end, then came the booming voice of Antonio Angelini. "Are you enjoying yourself?" he asked.

"Oh, yes, sir," came the deferential tone of Fred. "Thank you so much for all the wonderful things you've done for me. I'm the happiest I've ever been in my life, except for one thing." There was a long pause, then Fred continued. "There is this guy, Tom Johnson, who's always being rude to me at work, and I really wish I could get him to stop. Could you help me?" he asked, in a very subservient, pleading manner.

"I'll fix it," came the voice of Mr. Angelini, sounding much like the way a bowling ball does as it bounces down the gutter.

"Thank you so very much, sir," he said. "Thank you so very, very much."

It was raining the next morning, and Tom Johnson was literally shaking in his rubber boots. He met Fred Holcomb at the door and apologized profusely to Fred. He swore that he would never be rude again. He explained to Fred what had happened, that two men had paid him a short visit the night before and convinced him very quickly what a good idea it would be to apologize and change his behavior. He had a circle like a raccoon around one of his eyes, and it didn't take Fred long to figure out what had happened.

It was still pouring rain when Fred Holcomb pulled

his brand new Mercedes from his freshly painted private parking place that same afternoon. This afternoon, he decided to take the long way home to avoid the traffic. The rain was falling in sheets as he rounded the bend on the road where he first stopped to help Maria Angelini with her flat tire. Almost exactly in the same spot, he saw a car on the side of the road with steam rising up from under the hood like a metal, snorting dragon. He noticed the personalized license plate said "ANGEL" on it. Out of curiosity he slowed down and stopped, as the drenched old woman was trying in vain to get the hood up.

He put his finger on the console and lowered the power window on the passenger's side as the drenched old woman pleaded, "Please help me, will you please help me! I don't know anything at all about cars."

"Look, old woman," he said sarcastically, "I'm not ruining my new silk sport jacket just to get out and help you. Next time, get a better car that won't break down on you, or call on one of those angels like you have on your personalized license tag." Fred then floored the gas pedal and sent mud and water flying all over the helpless old woman. In the rearview mirror, he could see her surprised face as he chuckled to himself. His tag number, HST 273, probably didn't mean much to Fred, but to the woman, it was branded into her brain.

That night, Fred put on his red silk monogrammed pajamas and crawled into bed. That was also the night a thin man dressed in black crawled in through the bedroom window and put an ice pick through the monogram on the left breast pocket. Fred had chosen a good color to sleep in—the blood was barely noticeable.

Fred had made a fatal mistake. It wasn't just that he was cruel to a helpless old woman stranded on the side of the road. It wasn't just that he had made fun of her personalized "ANGEL" license tag or refused to help her. It was just that he had been disrespectful to Mrs. Rosa Angelini, the sainted mother of Antonio Angelini.

Well, as they say in Chicago, the gang lord giveth, and the gang lord taketh away.

28

Martha's Letter

The way to love anything is to realize it might be lost.

G. K. Chesterton

Paul Copeland is dark and wrinkled like a raisin. The crevices on his face have no patterns, as if time had plowed his face behind an unruly mule that chose its own course. He knows about mules, and soil, and crops, and hard work. He's been a farmer his whole life, but now, except for his small vegetable garden, he's retired and gets by on his Social Security check. Still, he's up at the rooster's crow and dressed in his overalls and boots. He is a man of ritual, always has been, and goes outside for his morning stroll around his house, checking the weather. His Vitalis-slicked hair doesn't move in the wind that carries his Old Spice scent to the deer in the nearby forest. He decides it won't rain, waters his garden and goes back inside the house where his daily ritual continues.

He takes his wife's picture from the mantel and dusts the glass with his red handkerchief. Convinced it is clean, he carefully places it back and, adjusting his bifocals, looks at the handful of books standing beside it. He pulls out the old family Bible he bought 30 years ago from a failed farmer turned Bible salesman. He sits in the rocker he made for Martha, his wife, and pulls out a letter that's more wrinkled than he. He reads:

Dear Paul,

I got to thinking the other day that most of us think we're going to live forever, but that just ain't true. I got to thinking that someday I might lose my mind like Grandma Barton did or die in my sleep like Aunt Grace, and I decided there were some things I wanted to say to you. I decided I'd better be getting that done, so I wrote this letter.

First of all, I want to say that I've always admired how hard you work. I remember the day that stubborn mule kicked you in the hand and broke your fingers. But you kept plowing until night came before you went over to Hillsboro and had Doc Johnson take care of you. I swear you're more stubborn than that mule was.

You helped me raise two fine boys and sent them to college. Can you actually believe that Bill and David are college graduates? I know you worked at the glove factory at night and farmed during the day, and they'll never know how much they owe you for your sacrifice. I darned your overalls so much they started looking like quilts, but you'd only laugh and say you weren't going to enter a fashion contest anyhow.

I want you to know that I have completely forgiven you for taking up with that loose woman over at the glove factory. You were just being an old fool, and when you came to your senses even you knew that. I know you weren't being mean. You were just looking to fill up some empty hole inside your heart that I never knew about. I remember you telling me that nothing could have grown in that dirt. You've got to have fine topsoil and that was what I was. Good Lord, Paul, only you could call me topsoil and make it seem like the greatest compliment I ever received. Anyway, thank you for wiping that cheap dirt off your feet.

Thank you for all the years of keeping me warm at night and safe from harm. Sometimes, I dream that we are young again and starting all over. I like that dream. I remember when we'd lay outside on a blanket and look at the stars. I felt like I'd burst wide open like a too-ripe watermelon in the sun. I used to pretend we'd be rich someday, with land as far as the eye could see. You'd have a whole passel of John Deere tractors moving like giants through the fields, and we'd have a big mansion with white columns.

Well, none of that came to be, and that's okay with me. It's been a fine life you've given me. I guess I've dreamed a lot in my life, but the truth is, I never dreamed I would live my life with such a wonderful man as you. I wouldn't trade it for anything in this whole wide world.

I love you,
Martha

Paul Copeland gently kisses the old letter and places it back in the Bible. Taking his red handkerchief again, he blots his blinking eyes, then shuffles over to the mantel and replaces the Bible above the fireplace. He knows how fortunate he is to have lived his life with such a fine woman as Martha. A man of ritual, he returns to the kitchen and makes a pot of coffee. He pours a cup and sweetens it until it tastes just right. Then he carries it down the hallway to the bedroom, where he sits down on the edge of the bed.

"Get up, Martha," he says, handing her the coffee. "We got a lot of fishing to do today!"

29

The Doctor
in the Dumpster

Nobody is too dumb to get sober, but
some are too smart.

Anonymous

Jeremy M. had it all. A big house, a beautiful wife, a big bank account, a big ego and a big position as a physician with a group of internists in upstate New York. Strangely, sometimes having it all isn't enough. So Jeremy experimented with drugs to make him feel even better. It wasn't too long before he had a big addiction to narcotics.

But Jeremy M. was one of those men who was too smart to get sober and straight. No one could help him because he didn't think he needed any help. After all, he won numerous prestigious scholarships, and who was as intelligent as he was? Jeremy wouldn't listen to his wife, but the divorce attorney did. He wouldn't listen to his medical partners, but the state medical board did. He lost his wife, his license, his money, and found himself with nothing but free time to pursue his addiction, which he did until he was dead broke. He crashed, not on Wall Street, but in the Bowery. He found out smartness can't keep you off skid row, and that's exactly where his addiction took him.

By now, Jeremy had changed. He no longer had the money for narcotics, so he took to alcohol. Soon he was a full-blown alcoholic. He grew a beard and took to wearing an old baseball hat, which he learned to belligerently stick out as he practiced the art of panhandling. He had lost all of his money but none of his false pride. He had one outfit of clothes and took to sleeping in the Dumpsters located in the alleys. He would crawl in and tie his shoes around his neck so no one would steal them

in his drunken sleep. Then he wrapped himself in news-
papers to stay warm. In the mornings, his body and
attitude both stank. Jeremy was resentful and angry at the
world, a world he once held in his hands.

Years went by him, and rivers of wine flowed through
him. One night, cold and hungry, he wandered into an
AA meeting. He didn't want sobriety; he wanted the hot
coffee and doughnuts. Before long, he was embroiled in
an argument, telling the group there was no proof of
God, and his intelligence was winning the debate. He was
disruptive, but they invited him to keep coming; no one
was dumb enough not to recognize he was a sick man.

Jeremy continued coming to AA and continued drinking also. He took no advice, just coffee and doughnuts.
One night, he proudly announced to the group that he
had been a doctor before he got a raw deal. But not a
soul actually believed him, except a kindly looking old
gentleman sitting in the back. After the meeting, the old
man asked Jeremy, "If you're so smart, and I do believe
you're a physician, why can't you stop drinking?"

Jeremy didn't even answer him. He stormed out of the
meeting and didn't come back the next week. He now
had added the AA group to the list of things he resented.
He didn't need them; his wine was what he needed.

After a couple of weeks, the old man saw him on the
street and invited him to come back. Jeremy cursed him,
but the man just smiled and said, "I'll come get you
tomorrow. Maybe it'll be a better meeting this time."

"I don't need you!" Jeremy spit out.

"Maybe not, but I need you. You see, you remind me
of me, and I can't very well reject myself, can I?" the
elderly man gently said. "Besides, I once was a medical
doctor myself. I lost my license during my last year of
practice, but you, Jeremy, you're still a young man."

"I don't need any help!" Jeremy screamed.

The white-haired man softly placed his hand on Jeremy's shoulder. "We physicians sure find it hard to believe the adage about not treating ourselves. For once, allow someone to help you. You do need help, Jeremy. I'll see you tomorrow. If you don't come, I'll see you the next day and every day after that until you come. I'm not giving up on you, so you might as well agree to humor me."

Jeremy had never seen anyone so persistent. He reluctantly agreed to go to the meeting the next day.

Jeremy went three months sober to prove to himself he didn't have a problem, and then he relapsed. He expected that would end his connection to AA, but it didn't. The old physician took him to a meeting the very next day.

This time, Jeremy stayed sober for an entire year. He emptied ashtrays, made coffee and put the chairs up after the meetings. He got honest and humble. He got the steps of AA, and they got him. He went to live with the old physician, and under his tutelage, Jeremy reapplied for his medical license. Over five years had passed since he lost his license, and he was informed he would have to take all the exams over again. For months, he studied day and night. He took the tests and passed, but it was a prayer of thanks, not pride, that followed the good news.

Jeremy M. once again became a licensed physician. His home AA group gave him a wonderful celebration. The wounded healer was healed by the powerful medicine of men and women struggling together with a common problem.

Jeremy has roots now. He runs a storefront medical practice on skid row, and he doesn't care whether his patients have insurance or not. He's giving back what he got, so he can keep it. That's the only kind of insurance he's interested in these days.

30
Mule Eggs

Everything is funny as long as it is
happening to someone else.

Will Rogers

Each morning they gather on the steps of the court-house at the town square of the small, rural Tennessee town. They come early and stay late. They are unique. They do two things. They whittle and tell stories.

Visitors and locals alike come to join these wonderful old men as they sit there in their overalls, whittling and carrying on the folklore tradition of yarns, tales, legends and very tall stories. Lawyers in three-piece suits carrying briefcases scurry up the steps to tell their tall stories inside the courthouse, but they would be no match for these flannel-clad masters with wits sharper than their knives, who sit on the outside, holding court. The white-haired elder statesman of the group clears his throat. It's time to begin. The others give him their undivided attention.

"Ever hear of mule eggs?" he asks the crowd with his eyebrows raised. They shake their heads no, and he smiles as he settles in to tell his story. "Well, once there was these two brothers, Esau and Thaddeus, who lived way up on a mountaintop isolated from most of civilization. The closest town was 40 miles away. They had been there only one time when they were small children, before their parents died, and they didn't remember much about it. Of course, they'd never been to school, and not being very bright, it probably wouldn't have done them much good anyway. But they knew how to hunt and farm, so they got along alright in their lonely existence, or at least they did until the day their plow mule died. That night, Esau and Thaddeus talked and decided there wasn't but one thing they could do.

They'd have to hitch up their old horse to the wagon and go down the mountain to that town and buy another mule. They took the last and only money they had, $50, and set out the next morning. After several days, they rolled into town and found the livery stable."

The storyteller's piece of wood is beginning to take on the shape of Abraham Lincoln's face. He pauses to blow off some shavings, then continues. "Esau and Thaddeus saw some mules in the owner's corral, so they asked the man, 'How much one of dem mules cost?' The owner asked, 'How much money you got?' They replied, 'We got $50.' The owner laughed. 'Boys, them mules cost $200 apiece. You can't get no mule for $50!' Esau turned to Thaddeus and said, 'Oh, well, we'uns done the best we could. We's best head back to the hills.'

"As they were leaving, Thaddeus saw a bunch of watermelons piled up in one corner of the stable. Since watermelons didn't grow up where he lived, he had never seen one before. 'What's dem thangs?' he asked the owner, who immediately realized he had two real rubes on his hands. 'Oh, those things,' he replied, 'they're mule eggs.'

"'How much dem cost?' Esau asked.

"'I hate to sell 'em,' the owner answered. 'But if I was to,' he said, followed by a long dramatic pause, 'I'd let you have one for $50.'

"'Mister, we'uns got to have a mule, and we'uns don't mind hatching our own. Please sell us one of dem mule eggs!' Thaddeus pleaded.

"'Well, seeing as how you two fellows seem to be nice and desperately need a mule, I'll let you have one,' the shrewd stableman replied.

"So, Thaddeus and Esau gave the man their $50. They put some straw down in the back of their wagon, carefully placed the watermelon on board and headed out. On the way back, they got into an argument as to who was going to sit on the mule egg until it hatched. They were about halfway home and still arguing when the wagon ran over a huge rut in the washed-out road and the watermelon fell from the wagon, splattering all over the road. A long-eared jackrabbit on the side of the road was startled by the plop of the watermelon and took off running up the road, past the wagon.

"'Looky thar!' Esau yelled to Thaddeus, pointing. 'Our mule egg's done hatched, and he's running up the road. We's got to catch him!'

"They both jumped down from the wagon and tore off after it. They ran as fast as they could, down one hollow and up the next, until they were slap worn out. Finally, Thaddeus, out of wind and sweating so bad that his overalls were soaked a dark blue, leaned against a tree and yelled for Esau to stop. 'Let him go, Esau! Let him go!' he hollered. 'I don't thank we'uns wants to plow that fast, no way!'"

The crowd laughs and claps its approval as the white-haired storyteller smiles and holds up his carving of Abraham Lincoln. "How much?" he asks the people as he auctions off his handiwork. Caught up in the spirit of the moment, I yell, "Fifty dollars." "Sold," he says, and hands me the carving.

Later on, I tour the small craft stores in the town square. A quaint shop has the same Lincoln carving for five dollars. Gossip really must travel fast in small towns. As I leave the shop, the storekeeper grins when he looks at my carving and says, "You must be the man who bought a mule egg."

31

The Inheritance

Where your treasure is, there will your heart be also.

Matt. 6:21

William Andrews turned 50 and turned for the worse. He felt his age but not much of anything else— except maybe forgotten—as it slowly dawned on him that he had gone as far as he could go in the company where he worked. He knew that he was never going to be an executive, that he was never going to make enough money to ease the financial pressure that strangled his sleep and, above all else, that he was never going to leave the position he had. He felt trapped, without enough strength to pull open the jaws of disillusionment, but he had invested too many years toward retirement to quit now. He was a passive passenger on a plane that had passed the point of no return, and he swore he would ride it out until it was all over. He also swore at those circumstances of life that had destined him never to sit in first class. Yet, despite his griping, he was essentially just one more man living a life of quiet desperation. Then came that telephone call to his home one Wednesday evening.

In solemn tones, the attorney told William the news. His Uncle Simon, his last living relative, had died. He did leave a widow, Louise, his third wife. "Unfortunately," the attorney said, "the poor thing's retarded and not competent enough to handle her affairs. As a result, your Uncle Simon made you the sole heir, with the provision that you allow Louise to come live with your family and take care of her basic needs. If you agree to this stipulation in writing, then I'll handle it from there. The will must be probated. It'll take about six months, but you'll need to come to Waco to sign the papers and pick up Louise in the meantime. I won't know how much you stand to inherit until we go through the probate process."

William and his wife, Della, were in Waco the next Monday morning, and by that evening, they were heading home with Aunt Louise safely sitting in the backseat. William had gone to the ranch to get her and had seen how large it was. He noticed the truck and the Lincoln Town Car in the garage. Although he had only seen a few of the prized pieces of the puzzle, he had already fashioned a beautiful box-top picture, and he was slap dab in the middle of it.

In the rearview mirror he saw the face of Aunt Louise. She was younger than Uncle Simon by almost 20 years and had that dazed look that death brings to those who are nearest. Her face was round, with her close-cropped hair making it appear even more so. She held her straw hat in her lap as she stared out the window without focusing. She was as lost as a small child sitting in a bus station late at night.

Several weeks went by, and each day William and Della told Aunt Louise to call them at their jobs if she needed them. They posted the numbers on the refrigerator with magnets, but she never called. She had other things to do. Each day, she cleaned the house until it was spotless, even though Della insisted that she rest. "No, you work," Aunt Louise said, "and I want to work, too."

Almost a month had passed, when William received a certified letter. The news was from the attorney and not good. Seems Uncle Simon hadn't paid income tax for the last 17 years, and the IRS had put a lien on every single thing he owned. The attorney said he was extremely sorry about the turn of events, but it appeared there would be no inheritance whatsoever. William felt he was the victim of a providential practical joke. He fumed and ranted, but none of it changed the words of the letter. William's resentments grew like watered weeds. "I'm stuck forever with Aunt Louise," he mumbled to himself.

One morning William lashed out at Della because he didn't have a clean, starched shirt to wear to work. It was a summer storm spat and over quickly, but that afternoon when they got home from work, they found Aunt Louise smiling like a three-year-old with a secret too big to hide. When William went to the bedroom to change clothes, he saw why. Every dress shirt he owned had been washed, starched and ironed as though a professional cleaner had done the work. He just stood there before the open closet and maybe would have smiled if his resentments could have loosened their hold on his lips. The best he could manage was a "Thank you" to Aunt Louise at the supper table and a brief "You don't need to do that anymore" to ward off the guilt feelings that were surfacing. She smiled big.

William shouldn't have complained about his brown shoes being scuffed the next morning. For when he got home from work and opened his closet, he saw that every last shoe he owned had been polished to such a sheen that they reflected the closet light. He never thought his old work boots would shine again, but he was wrong. He was wrong about something else also, but he simply wouldn't admit it to himself.

Every day, when William and Della came home from work, they found Aunt Louise had done something else, especially those tasks that they complained about. One day, she cooked William's favorite meal, fried chicken, and it was good enough to bring shame to the famous face of Colonel Sanders. Once, she even cut the lawn, front and back. But that wasn't all. She had trimmed the hedges, edged the walk and made a rock garden out back by the carport. One night at supper, one that Aunt Louise had cooked, William asked her, "Aunt Louise, why do you keep doing all of this for us? I mean, you do so much, you know."

Aunt Louise nervously rubbed her fingers, then she smiled that childlike Christmas-morning smile. It was as though she had just unwrapped a special thought and wanted William and Della to hold it.

"Oh my," she said bashfully. "Ya'll took me in when I had no place to go. Why, there's not a thing in this world I wouldn't do for ya'll." She glanced down at her hands and continued. "Besides, I just do these things because I love ya'll, and it makes my heart sing to be able to help."

William reached across the table and squeezed her hand. "You're part of this family, Aunt Louise, and we love you, too."

Aunt Louise jumped up from her chair as though she'd spilled hot coffee in her lap and literally ran to her room. She returned clutching a folded piece of paper in her hand. "Simon said the day I heard ya'll say you loved me, I was to give ya'll this. I'm so happy," she said. "Well, here it is." She gave the piece of paper to William. It was a check.

That was the evening that William realized that he had been humbled by love and kindness. That was the evening when he knew for certain that God had sent Aunt Louise to teach him some lessons about life.

You see, that evening when William unfolded the check, he realized it was blank except for some words Uncle Simon had written on the back of it. "Dear William," it said, "By now I know you know the truth, that this check is worthless and Louise is priceless. Take good care of her. She is an angel disguised in human form. P.S. Fill in any amount of anything you want but money. Life really is a blank check, you know. With love, Uncle Simon." William grinned, for now he knew.

32

An Extra Place
at the Table

The way of God is complex; He is hard
for us to predict. He moves the pieces,
and they come somehow into a kind of
order.

Euripides

Jonathan lived in the country, where life was slow. That suited him just fine because he was slow, too. At least, that is what his grandpa, Samuel Ellis, had always laughingly told him when he didn't snap to it and do the chores as he was told. However, Grandma Myra always said he was special and being slow was a good thing because it made you really think before you acted, so you didn't make dumb mistakes like those smart-aleck kids who were always getting into trouble. Jonathan liked his grandma's version of what being mentally slow meant a lot better than his grandpa's, even though he knew Grandpa was only kidding.

Grandma and Grandpa Ellis had raised him since he was seven years old. Jonathan's mother and father were killed in a car accident. The accident left Jonathan with a severe head injury that altered his thinking and a heart injury that Samuel and Myra healed with that powerful potion called love.

Jonathan was a chunky 15-year-old, and when he laughed, his eyes almost squinted shut, as though the sun were forever shining in his eyes. He was a kind boy living a simple life that summer of 1995.

His grandpa had brought Jonathan a dog when Jonathan was 11. It was a hound dog, and when Grandpa Ellis returned to the house, he announced to all that the dog's name was Homer. Grandma wanted to know if that would be the Homer who wrote the *Iliad*. Jonathan said he thought that perhaps Grandpa had named him that because that was the best you could do in baseball.

Grandpa only smiled and said that the name came from the fact that that was the puppy he decided to take home, and hence the name *Homer*. Well, it made no difference the source of the name; they all loved Homer just the same.

One Saturday afternoon, Jonathan walked down the winding road to the mailbox to "fetch" the mail for Grandma Myra. He had whistled for Homer to come and be with him, but he couldn't find him. Down near the mailbox, he saw Homer all curled up like he was sleeping, but he didn't move when Jonathan called his name. Homer had been playing near the road when some cruel person drove past and shot him with a pistol. A tiny stream of blood flowed from Homer's left ear, where the bullet had entered his trusting head, killing him.

With panic on his face, Jonathan ran back to the house with Homer nestled in his chubby arms. Grandma hurriedly rang the dinner bell on the back porch, and Grandpa Ellis was there in a few minutes, sitting on the tractor he was using to turn the fields. When he saw what had happened, he jumped down with the engine still running. There was nothing he could do but hold Jonathan close to him and look at Myra as if he were a lost little boy himself, just like Jonathan.

That evening, Grandpa Ellis dug a grave near the house because Jonathan said Homer might get afraid in the night if he wasn't near the ones he loved. They fashioned a cross out of two sturdy sticks and placed it at the head of the fresh grave. The sun seemed so heavy with sadness that it drooped lower and lower until finally night came to help shield their eyes from the coarse reality of that awful day. Even the night brought its own brand of tears as the dew fell softly.

The next morning, Grandma and Grandpa Ellis were

sitting at the kitchen table, eating breakfast and looking out the raised kitchen window as Jonathan stood quietly beside the grave. The biscuits stuck in their throats as they heard Jonathan speak, with his head facing the morning sky.

"God, I ain't too smart, so I need an answer I can understand," he said, as the soft morning breeze blew through the magnolia tree. "You see, I love Homer, and I miss him so very much. He looked so natural yesterday, just like he was sleeping. I sure wish he hadda been just sleeping. It's this way, God: Homer never hurt nobody, and he always came when you called him, and I don't understand how anybody in this world could have hurt Homer." Jonathan's eyes squinted at the morning sun, but this time he wasn't laughing. He was crying, and his chubby body shook unashamedly.

"Homer was my best friend, God," he said. "He loved me even when I forgot to feed him or give him new water. He never thought I was slow. He knew I'd do it as soon as I could remember to. I'm sorry, God, that he had to wait on me to remember. But I never forgot how he felt in my arms when he licked my face to wake me up in the mornings. I never forgot how he met me at the bus when I got home from school. I'll never forget how we played and explored stuff. You see, God, Homer never forgot me, and I can't forget him," Jonathan said, as his tears fell and mixed with the dew.

"You see, God, there's this empty place in my heart that's shaped just like Homer, and it hurts 'cause he's not there anymore. But I don't want you to think I am complaining, God, 'cause I ain't. You see, I guess I hurt so much 'cause I loved Homer so much. I guess I wouldn't be so sad if I hadn't loved him more than anything in this whole world. Maybe this giant sadness is what it cost me to have a giant love, and if that is so, God, I reckon it was worth it. Oh, I almost forgot my question, God. I was wondering if dogs get to go to Heaven. 'Cause if they don't, I'm not coming."

Grandpa Ellis swallowed hard, but Grandma could only cry as she sat at the kitchen table. That was the week that Samuel Ellis told Jonathan that of course, Homer would be going to Heaven because wasn't it true that "God" was "dog" spelled backwards? It was not a very sophisticated answer, but Jonathan sure liked it. He smiled a knowing smile, as if that settled the matter. But the matter wasn't settled.

The following Saturday, one week to the day, Jonathan trudged down to "fetch" the mail for Grandma Ellis. He had just pulled the lid down and was reaching for the mail when he heard a rustle in the shrubbery near the mailbox. He dropped down on his hands and knees to get a better look. Peering into the thick growth, he saw the source of the movement—it was a hound dog puppy. His eyes squinted shut as he laughed with joy. He coaxed the baby puppy out, placed him in his chubby arms, then tore up the road, yelling, "Grandma Ellis, come here! Look! Quick, come here!"

She came out onto the front porch, wiping her hands on her apron. "Why, my goodness, Jonathan, what do we have here? It looks like a baby Homer!"

"He does, he does!" Jonathan squealed. "Look, Grandma! God brought me a new Homer. I found him in the bushes near the road." Jonathan quickly cocked his head to one side and then said, "I just remembered, Grandma. I'll get him some new water." He started toward the water spigot, then stopped, turned around and said, "This must be Homer's baby. I bet him and God are watching to see if I remember better this time." He hurried off to get the water.

Grandma stood there watching as her grandson and the dog frolicked together. She also had been watching from her rocker on the front porch earlier that morning, when an old pickup truck stopped on the side of the road, the door opened, and one more unwanted puppy was abandoned on the roadside by an uncaring person.

She thought of how a cruel person had killed Homer and brought Jonathan so much heartache, and how a cruel person had brought the cure for his heartache. It was just too complicated and confusing to try to figure it all out. What she did know was that the events were just too wondrous to be coincidental.

Grinning, she winked to the heavens, straightened her apron and went back to fixing lunch. The presence of God was so strong that she even set an extra place at the table that day.

About the Author

John M. Eades, Ph.D., lives in Winchester, Tennessee, and is the outreach marketing director for a geriatrics program located at Columbia Southern Tennessee Medical Center. He is a 20-year veteran in the field of addictive disease counseling and has served as chemical dependency director for several major hospitals. He is an accomplished public speaker and has addressed numerous conventions and professional organizations. He strives to bring inspiration and humor to the many topics he covers in his presentations.

New from the *Chicken Soup for the Soul*® Series

Chicken Soup for the Teenage Soul

Teens welcome *Chicken Soup for the Teenage Soul* like a good friend: one who understands their feelings, is there for them when needed and cheers them up when things are looking down. A wonderful gift for your teenage son, daughter, grandchild, student, friend... #4630—$12.95

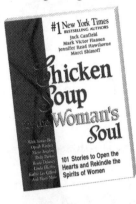

Chicken Soup for the Woman's Soul

The #1 *New York Times* bestseller guaranteed to inspire women with wisdom and insights that are uniquely feminine and always from the heart. #4150—$12.95

Chicken Soup for the Christian Soul

Chicken Soup for the Christian Soul is an inspiring reminder that we are never alone or without hope, no matter how challenging or difficult our life may seem. In God we find hope, healing, comfort and love. #5017—$12.95

Chicken Soup for the Soul® Series

Each one of these inspiring *New York Times* bestsellers brings you exceptional stories, tales and verses guaranteed to lift your spirits, soothe your soul and warm your heart! A perfect gift for anyone you love, including yourself!

A 4th Course of Chicken Soup for the Soul, #4592—$12.95
A 3rd Serving of Chicken Soup for the Soul, #3790—$12.95
A 2nd Helping of Chicken Soup for the Soul, #3316—$12.95
Chicken Soup for the Soul, #262X—$12.95

Selected books are also available in hardcover, large print, audiocassette and compact disc.

Available in bookstores everywhere or call **1-800-441-5569** for Visa or MasterCard orders. Prices do not include shipping and handling. Your response code is **BKS**.